MAID'S HEAD TO HAMBURG

'I'm just the drummer in the band'

RICK MEEK

**THIS BOOK IS DEDICATED TO MY GOOD FRIEND
AND FELLOW DRUMMER
BARRIE 'B J' WILSON (1947 – 1990)**

'Remembering the good times buddy'

Published by
Berimbau Music

First published
2007

Origination, printing and binding by
Paris Print & Design
Crescent Lane
Hunstanton PE36 5BX

© R. Meek 2007

The moral right of the author has been asserted

British Library Cataloguing in Publication Data
A catalogue record for this book is available from the British Library

ISBN
978-0-9556001-0-4

Contents

		Page
Chapter 1.	Mr Beat (May 1943 – Dec 1958)	1
Chapter 2.	Talking Turkey to Mr Beat! (Jan 1959 – Oct 1962)	5
Chapter 3.	Mike Prior & The Escorts (Nov 1962 – April 1963)	9
Chapter 4.	Mixing Paint With Pasadena! (April 1963 – Nov 1963)	13
Chapter 5.	Can It Really Be Hamburg? (Nov 1963 – Jan 1964)	18
Chapter 6.	Hamburg Days (Feb 1964)	21
Chapter 7.	Riding On A High (Mar 1964 – Nov 1964)	39
Chapter 8.	Rock Bottom (Nov 1964 – Mar 1965)	44
Chapter 9.	Finding My Way Back (April 1965 – Oct 1970)	47
Chapter 10.	Picking Up The Pieces (The 1970's)	52
Chapter 11.	Still Rockin' After All These Years (The 1980's & Beyond)	73
Chapter 12.	Bringing The Music Up To Date (1992 – 2006)	78
	Thanks Maids Head to Hamburg	81
	My Top Ten Lists and Bibliography	83
	Photo Credits	87

Chapter One – Mr Beat (May 1943 – December 1958)

I was born on May 31st 1943 in the old King's Lynn General Hospital, Norfolk. A Gemini (the twins) – a star sign that would prove true throughout my life, there has always been two sides to my genetic make up, but more of that later on in the story.
An only child I was named Richard Odo Meek, my middle name in memory of my great uncle Odo, my grandmother's brother (on my mother's side). As a child I came to detest this name as I was always being teased at school and as I grew older got fed up with always being questioned about its origins. I researched the name but the only real gem of information I gleaned, that there was a King Odo in the 8th century, but nobody it seemed had ever heard of him! In due course I dropped my middle name and have not used it since my school days.
I lived in Dersingham, Norfolk with my parents for the first twenty two years of my life. They in turn had moved there in 1938, first renting before finally buying the property in the mid 1950's.
My father Eric Alan Meek was born in Snettisham, Norfolk on December 8th 1912, the youngest of three brothers whose parents were Mr & Mrs William Meek (my grandfather was born in 1864, my grandmother I think around 1870/71) who owned the local grocery store in the village market place. His brothers were much older and I never really knew them or my grandparents, who had both died by the time I reached two years old.
My dad was a talented musician, by his teens he was a proficient violinist playing in local orchestras in the area. He later went on to play the double bass, mandolin, banjo and many other string instruments and worked in some of the local pre-war dance bands. After the war he was a member of Hank, Luke & Lofty, later to be known as the Snettisham Hill Billy Band, a very successful country band, particularly from the late 1940's through the 1950's with appearances on radio's 'Opportunity Knocks' and stage shows around the theatres. His stage name was 'Lofty' Meek and the name stuck for the remainder of his life. He was even made a honorary Deputy Marshall of Tombstone City, Arizona, when an American Serviceman stationed I think at USAF Sculthorpe took a tape of the band back home with him and the local Sheriff showed interest in them. He tried to get the band some cowboy boots, but you couldn't export anything like that in the 50's, so he made the band honorary Deputy Marshall's instead!
My dad also had a fine singing voice (something he didn't hand down to me) and although various personnel came and went he kept a band together until he had reached his early seventies, he was well respected and liked by fellow musicians and audiences alike and he was to play a big part in encouraging my early musical career.
My mother Nina Felice Williams, like me an only child, was born May 1st 1913 to Richard (born in 1879) and Lily (born 1881) Williams of Shernbourne, Norfolk. They were originally from Gloucestershire, but moved to Norfolk when my grandfather, a Gamekeeper was offered a position as Royal Gamekeeper on the Sandringham Estate. He looked after the pheasant beat for both King George V and King George VI, and he spent many hours with the Royal Family and told illuminating stories of his times with them. My grandfather had the rather daunting task of teaching Queen Elizabeth (the late Queen Mother) to shoot on one of her early visits to Sandringham. A fact she

never forgot, as she recalled many years later to my grandmother when they met up at a Christmas gathering at Sandringham, not long before my grandmother's death in 1985.

My grandfather had served in the Army in the South African Campaign of 1908 and was wounded in battle. Sadly he was to die just two years into his retirement in 1948, but I do recollect a memory of him visiting me during the heavy snow of 1947 with snow glistening on his boots!

My mum and dad met at a dance in about 1934, they were married on September 26th 1936 at Shernbourne and began married life living with my dad's parents at Snettisham, where both my parents helped out in the family shop.

Not long after the war was declared in September 1939 my dad was called to serve his Country and like many young men at that time would be the first occasion he had left home. He joined the RAF, nothing as exciting as a fighter pilot, but mundane office work, which took him to RAF bases as far apart as Oxfordshire and Northumberland. My mum was able to join him for a period of time when stationed near Morpeth, not far from the Scottish borders, but for a greater part of the war they were often apart. After the war ended he took an office job at RAF Bircham Newton (now the Construction Training College). He later spent time working for the Inland Revenue and West Norfolk Fertilisers, King's Lynn (the old 'Muck Works') as Wages Clerk, before buying a newsagents shop in St.James Street, King's Lynn. He later sold the shop and worked part time looking after the office of a local camera shop before retiring in 1977, but continued with his band until about 1984.

My childhood was quite idyllic and sheltered compared to today's world, I don't remember the war I was only 2 years old when it ended. We had no TV until I was 12 years old. Childhood was a happy time spent with lots of friends who met up on the village common to chat, play football and various long forgotten games not known to today's children. I looked forward to the occasional day trip to the coast, settling in the back of my dad's old Ford 8 to visit Hunstanton or Wells-next the-Sea, building sand castles and eating ice cream.

I had to cope with a childhood stammer, which was not a condition that was highly prioritised for treatment in the early 1950's, although I did receive some speech therapy. This knocked my confidence somewhat and only those with a similar impediment can fully appreciate what a devastating effect it can have when even the simplest tasks, such as asking for an item in a shop or stating your destination on a bus, become almost impossible for fear of stammering. I once walked out on a job interview in case I couldn't get my address details out without a stammer. Over the years I have managed to virtually overcome this problem and found ways to hide it, and today my stammer only intermittently crops up. I think my early interest in music was a way of expressing my thoughts without the need of having to speak to people directly and certainly once I began playing in a band I overcame any previous nerves and became much more self-confident.

Around 8years old I became interested in music. I had been to a couple of local dances where dad had played and I became fascinated with drums and guitar. This was 1951/2. My mum thought I should learn to play the piano, so I went for lessons with a music teacher in the next village and I found the whole experience utterly boring. I learnt to sight read a bit and to play endless scales but in the end much to my mum's disappointment I quit. I wanted to play real tunes like dad, and the ones I'd heard on radio's 'Two Way Family Favourites' and 'Billy Cotton's Band Show'. So apart from the occasional chance to see dad's band, music remained in the background for the next three or four years. My interest resumed when dad brought home an acoustic guitar and after a little persuasion he showed me a few chords. I would be 12/13 years old at the time and rock 'n' roll was in its early infancy (Bill Haley, Elvis etc). From the money I had saved from odd jobs I bought one of the early transistor radios and soon found Radio Luxemburg, the only radio station that constantly played the latest American pop. I later bought a guitar and self-taught myself as many chords, in as many keys as I could find. My guitar/singing debut was at the Dukes Head Hotel, King's Lynn, probably around 1957 singing two or three songs (I can only remember *The Yellow Rose of Texas*) with dad's band.

Although my mum was always very supportive in all my musical accomplishments, she had little interest in popular music, but she was a fine musician in her own right playing both the piano and church organ. She preferred classical and organ music throughout her life, but I know she would love to tell her friends all about my musical exploits particularly when I was in Hamburg.

After my grandfather's death my grandmother lived in a 'grace and favour' bungalow on the Sandringham Estate, and played host to many visits from the Royal Family when they visited Sandringham. She loved to tell the story of when the young Prince Charles and Princess Anne cycled over from Sandringham House and rode around her lawn, also when Queen Elizabeth called in one afternoon with one of her corgis and asked gran for a bowl of water for the royal dog. As a child I also met some of the Royal Family and I well recall meeting the late Queen Mary on one of her visits. I often saw the Spencer family who lived at nearby Park House. In the 1960's I little thought that the small girl playing in the park with her sisters and brother would one day become, Diana, Princess of Wales and die such a tragic death. I also remember one evening being locked in the park and Lord Spencer letting me through the grounds of Park House to aid my escape!

My gran's next door neighbour was Lala Bill who had been a Royal Nanny. She is mentioned in several books written about the Royal Family. In 2003 her story was told in the BBC production 'The Lost Prince'. Her real name was Charlotte Bill and I spent many an hour chatting to her about her life with the Royal Family and her world travels, I still have postcards from her that she sent from various exotic locations. Although she never married, the Royal Family always referred to her as 'Mrs Bill', which was a courtesy title bestowed on her. She was a very down to earth lady who always downplayed her Royal connection

My gran loved to sing and listened to all the latest pop music, she always had her radio on and on my weekend visits to her in the late 1950's I would catch her listening to BBC's 'Saturday Morning Club' and the 'Skiffle Club'. Gran loved early Cliff Richard, Lonnie Donegan, Elvis and the Everly Brothers. Although never having any formal piano lessons she would pick the tunes out on the piano and proudly play the latest No 1, and a lot of her enthusiasm and love of music would pass down to me. She was my number one fan and kept all the many newspaper clippings, and was especially proud to see the Escorts name in TV Times when we appeared on 'Junior Angle Club' in 1963.

My schooldays passed by very quickly, I attended Dersingham Primary School (1948-1954) and then on to St.Georges Secondary Modern (1954 – 1958) which was also in Dersingham. I was quite bright, but probably lazy and I failed my eleven plus and did not sit for any O or A levels. In fact my only achievements were the senior geography prize (I've always loved travelling) and the school award for consideration and helpfulness (must have licked round somebody). I was also a school prefect, all of these accolades were obtained in my final year. I enjoyed geography, history and English, but hated PE and woodwork/metalwork; I must have been the only kid in the class who made a rounded wooden fruit bowl almost square! Strangely I never did that well in music. I did make my debut as a drummer at an end of term concert in 1957, when the kid who was supposed to play with year 4's Skiffle band had last minute nerves and dropped out. I volunteered and although I'd never played before was a surprise hit (I should have dropped the guitar back then). I put my problem with the music class down to the fact that the music teacher was of the 'old school' strictly classical, and she frowned on my guitar playing and pop interest. However I did please her and attended several classical concerts that were held regularly for schools at the Guildhall, King's Lynn (I hadn't the heart to tell her this was purely to get out of other lessons). Years later I met up with my old music teacher and she did in fact congratulate me on my musical achievements, so perhaps she liked me after all!

On leaving school in July 1958 I was offered a trainee clerk's job with a local Solicitor or a position at the 'Muck Works' ......wait for it!, as a office junior with chances of promotion after a year. The weekly wage was a staggering £2.17.6d - of course I took the job at the 'Muck Works', because I could travel to work with my dad!

I still continued trying to master the guitar, but gave up the idea of ever playing lead guitar and concentrated on rhythm, going out from time to time with dad's band.

Although my mum and dad were musicians they never listened to any music and never owned a record player of any description. I used to go round to a friend's house and listen to early rock 'n' roll records that his parents had bought him and soon grew to love Bill Haley, Gene Vincent, Everly Brothers, Chuck Berry, Jerry Lee Lewis, Little Richard and Fats Domino. Back then; I always seem to prefer American artists and recordings to British and my love for all this great music has never diminished!

I really wanted a record player of my own and on telling my friend Norman, who lived a couple of doors away, he came up with a brilliant idea. He had seen an advert in a newspaper for a self assembly record deck kit, so cheap I can't even remember what the cost was. I soon sent off for one, all we had to do was screw it all to a solid wooden board, then connect it to the radio amplifier and speaker. This we did after a lot of effort and great it worked. About this time I became mad about jazz, still my favourite music (see the Gemini creeping in). A guy from Snettisham, I can't remember his name, lent me some Sonny Rollins, John Coltrane and Thelonious Monk records and I was hooked. So some of the first records I bought were jazz – Stan Getz's 'Imported From Europe' was one and I loved Chris Barber's 'Elite Syncopations'. I got totally hooked on the drumming on the latter which was Graham Burbidge. I got the opportunity in the early 1970's to tell Graham, when I worked with Chris Barber a few times.

Of course I bought a few singles such as Buddy Holly & The Crickets, Rick Nelson and Roy Orbison.. I also started my love of blues and sort out Ray Charles, Muddy Waters and Charles Brown.

I still wasn't playing drums as 1958 came to an end, but I was becoming more involved with music, listening to a mixed bag of current pop, blues and jazz. Trad (traditional jazz), New Orleans style Dixieland was beginning to grab the attention of the younger duffle coated crowd and Corn Exchanges up and down the country would soon be echoing to the sounds of Terry Lightfoot, Acker Bilk, Chris Barber, Bob Wallis and the many others that toured the circuit – so on to 1959.

Chapter Two – Talking Turkey to Mr Beat! (January 1959 – October 1962)

The only really exciting thing that happened during the first half of 1959 was buying a motorbike just after my sixteenth birthday. I used to ride pillion on a friend's bike and during the winter months had gone to a few dances around the area such as East Dereham, where drummer Paul Chris and his band often used to play, and other popular dance venues that included the Assembly Rooms, Swaffham and the now demolished Sandringham Ballroom (Casino), Hunstanton.

Although I dreamed of BSA Gold Star's my machine was a rather humble Ambassador 200cc, but it did give me wheels! I put in for my test and passed first time later that year.

In the summer I first met a young guitarist named Michael Williamson. Mike had contacted my father to see if he could do any work with the band and we both went to a gig at the Guildhall, King's Lynn. Mike was a good rhythm player who also played some lead as well. We soon became friends and in the 70's we would work together in several band permutations.

I had fitted a pick up on my trusty Hofner acoustic which I ran through an old second hand amp. I was never pleased with the sound, so I decided to get a new Hofner solid body and amp. I sold my old guitar to a friend of my father's and picked up my new gear from Wheelers, the local music shop in King's Lynn. I met up with Mike Williamson a few times where we would practice some Shadow's numbers, my rhythm to Mike's lead, I can't remember too much about these sessions, it probably sounded bloody awful! Mike went on to join King's Lynn band the Trojans who became quite popular during the early 60's

Another event that happened during the year was Anglia TV's promotion in East Anglia. The ITV station opened towards the end of the year, but in the lead up to this they had a road show that visited all the major towns in the area and in due course set up shop in the Corn Exchange, King's Lynn for a weekend. They brought with them all the TV cameras, lights, sound equipment and other gear and made a kind of studio with monitors etc., local bands were invited to perform in front of the cameras, which provided free entertainment for the hundreds of visitors that came to gaze at the screens. I went along with dad, and the band performed for half an hour or so, this was great fun and I remember a young Susan Hampshire introducing all the bands. She worked for Anglia TV for a short time before starting her acting career and becoming the famous actress she is today.

The only other band that I recall was Paul Chris, who put on a great show, but there were quite a few more there and it has stuck in my memory.

The year rolled by quite quickly, but the highlight for me was to go to Heacham Public Hall to hear the visiting trad jazz bands. It was always packed out and people used to travel miles to see the bands. Heacham attracted the top names at the time including Bob Wallis, Terry Lightfoot, Dick Charlesworth & His City Gents, and many more. I would always be watching the drummers, I was a natural timekeeper and loved the way these musicians 'traded fours' (taking four bars solo) and I think I knew even then that one day I would become a drummer.

It was during this time that I dropped using Richard as my first name and became known as 'Ricky' or 'Rick', and to a few close friends I am known as 'Dick' (very confusing I know). I always felt Richard was too formal and I've never endorsed any formalities if I could get away with it.

The promises made by the 'Muck Works' of promotion and better pay were as far as I was concerned just false promises. I had worked hard and even gone to evening classes to better my maths and took a course in business studies. Several jobs had come up for grabs, I always applied, but the answer was the same each time, 'when the right job comes along we'll consider you'. So by the summer of 1960 I got fed up and started to look round for other jobs. I had gone to John Colliers, the High St tailors for a new suit and had got in conversation with the manager Ivan Dunbabin about music and it turned out he was a bass player. I mentioned my despondency with my job and he said Colliers were always looking for trainees, so I wrote to the area office, had an interview and was offered a job starting in King's Lynn, but I would be expected to move to other branches in due course - and yes those magic words were talked about 'promotion and more pay' plus a new phrase uttered by the area manager 'we'll talk turkey'. Even today I'm not too sure what it means, but it sure as hell didn't mean what I though it meant as I was to find out in time.

I enjoyed the job, even though I had to work on a Saturday. Ivan was a nice guy and in quieter moments we would chat about music, he didn't like pop, but was quite happy to tell me about his gigs with a local dance band. I also got to know Tommy Thurston, who worked for Alexander's, he played trumpet with the Paul Chris Band, and tragically he died in a horrific car accident not long after we'd met. The prominent High St clothing shops in King's Lynn such as John Colliers, Alexander's, Weaver To Wearer and Hepworths all seem to attract musicians and besides Ivan, Tommy and myself others included drummers Dennis Scott and Alan Lockwood.

In the October I was sent to the Peterborough branch of Collier's for a couple of months. I lodged with a nice old couple just off the city centre. I soon found money very tight, I wasn't being paid any extra, but decided to make the best of it. The only music I could find was at the various clubs that were run by the brick companies, engineering factories etc. A guy at work took me to one club, which had an organ trio playing quicksteps, so I quickly beat a hasty retreat and couldn't wait to get back home.

In early 1961 I was sent to a permanent position at one of the Norwich branches of John Colliers. I jumped at the chance; even back then Norwich was a pretty happening city with bags of good music. The area manager 'talked turkey' again and promised if I could manage the first month on my old pay, this would be increased by more than enough to pay lodging and make it worthwhile. I had been given money at Christmas for driving lessons, so I soon set about learning in an Austin A40, quite a modern car then. I enjoyed driving through the city and passed my test first time in King's Lynn later in the year.

The cleaner at the shop also did some cleaning at Anglia TV and she was talking to me one day about a talent competition Anglia were organising, so I got an application form and sent it in. I entered as a country guitarist/singer; I arranged four Hank Williams songs as a medley and practised them.

I travelled down to a theatre in Lowestoft on my day off for my audition. I thought it went off okay, didn't break any strings or forget any words, but I still received a letter of rejection a couple of weeks later, but as many a future star would say I only did it for the experience!

If I had enough money left over I would go and hear some jazz and I remember seeing Ken Colyer and Sandy Brown in the spring of 1961. I also used to go to a couple of pubs that had live music, mostly folk, tinged with the blues.

Money was becoming a major problem; my mum and gran bailed me out a time or two. I promised to pay them back just as soon as my pay increase came through, but one month turned into two and then three and still there was no extra cash. I told my shop manager of my financial crisis, he reassured me and said he would speak to the area manager. One day when I had been in Norwich for almost four months the area manager made his monthly visit, as I had heard nothing I tackled him head on, instead of the response I expected, he told me if I wasn't satisfied go find another job, where was all the 'talking turkey'. I flipped and told him what he could do with his job and quit. After being let down twice I had learnt a valuable lesson in life, never believe everything you're told or trust employers to be honest. To this day I don't suffer fools gladly or accept any unfairness to me or to others, and most importantly I learnt how to work to my own advantage as much as possible, certainly not the other way round.

I came back home a little disillusioned, it was the middle of May. I took a week off and applied for a job in the boy's clothing department of Catleughs in King's Lynn, and got it. Catleughs was almost a spin off for TV's 'Are You Being Served', which had yet to be devised. Andy Archer (who went on to work at Radio Caroline and Radio Norfolk) was another 'face' that served time in the boy's department during the early 60's; I think some time after me.

It was in the autumn that I met up with guitarist John Nockolds and drummer Dennis Scott, we even had a couple of sessions playing probably Shadow's numbers, I can't really remember now. During the months ahead I still occasionally went out with my dad's band, but I was losing interest in playing guitar and I was never going to be a great singer. I started to visit the now demolished Kit-Kat at Hunstanton. I had been there a few times when dad played there, they were slowly changing their music policy, out went the dance bands and solo organists to be replaced by local beat groups as they were known back then. On Sunday nights the place was packed with local teenagers who came to see the Offbeats led by drummer Nigel Portass. Today he is better known for his keyboards, but back in late '61 early '62 Nigel was and still is, a hell of a drummer and I used to watch him closely. At various Youth Clubs in the area bands like the Strangers were also getting pretty popular and I became hooked on this music.

In the summer of '62, I got the chance to play the drums of a friend and I finally realised I could be a drummer and I started to get serious thoughts to putting all my energies into drumming.

It took a series of events to act as a wake up call and get me to buy a kit and get started. Firstly I felt I was still in a going nowhere job which was getting me down and I started to take days off, plus I had a few personal problems that I had to deal with. All of this came to a head in August, the result was I quit my job, made up my mind to concentrate on music full time and took my guitar and amp to Wheelers and traded them in as a deposit on a red sparkle Edgeware drum kit. I added some Super-Zyn hi-hats and a ride cymbal, plus a Zyn crash cymbal and cases and covers. I pleaded with my dad to sign the loan agreement (the legal age then was 21) and reluctantly he did. At last I was ready to show the world I was going to be a great drummer!

I had sold my motorbike earlier in the year and with that money and some my gran gave me I bought an old Austin Devon, which was just big enough to get all my drum kit in.

I soon set about practising, I had a daily routine that began just after breakfast and apart from lunch I continued through the day, often playing 8/10 hours a day (I must have driven my mother crazy and the neighbours too). My main source for technique was listening to drummers on records plus all the tips I'd picked up from watching drummers through the years. Without sounding boastful, I was a natural drummer and had a good 'ear'. I also understood rhythm and timing. I could listen to a particular song and hear what the drummer was doing and then translate it more or less straight away, adding my own inflections and interpretation. Later as I taught myself more and improved my technique, I practised less at home. I am completely a self-taught drummer, but I have always listened and watched other drummers throughout my life. I think drummers fall into two distinct categories – and it doesn't matter to some extent what skills they have learned, or how long they may have been playing, they either play completely for themselves and don't listen to the music being played by the other musicians, play at one volume, usually 'loud' and have nothing left for 'accents'. Or thank goodness just the opposite, they listen to everything happening around them, hearing all the 'changes' and 'accents', so they can drive everything along to make the end result worth listening to. Also one of my pet hates is the 'tippy-tappy' drummer who just taps along to a tune. Drums are made to be hit, hard at times and you must coax the tones out of a drum if you are ever to get a good solid sound and you must take the trouble to tune your drums to make the overall sound dynamic and musically interesting.

I felt confident by the end of September to look around for a band, not just any band, but a group of like minded individuals like myself who wanted to play today's music. There were not a lot of drummers around and those that were any good were already in a band. This was very much a cross-over time for music, the older style dance bands, which included my dad's were still in demand and playing for lots of dances, but a younger audience were demanding modern sounds. Rock 'n' roll had been around since the mid 50's, but with new dance numbers such as the 'twist' and an abundance of record releases from new groups, solo singers and instrumentalists from both sides of the Atlantic, Youth Clubs and young entrepreneurs were putting on dances aimed at a new audience. The dances at the Kit-Kat at Hunstanton were so successful that by the autumn of 1962, it was so packed out they had to open the ground floor to guest groups.

At first I didn't have much luck, I knew most of the groups in the area and they all had existing drummers, I even had a few jam sessions with among others, guitarist Tony Pull who at that time was with the Strangers and Mike Donald from the Paul Chris Band. In fact my first professional gig as a drummer was October 27th 1962 at a wedding playing along with just an organist, hardly the debut I had envisioned. It was not very challenging or exciting but at least I could play all those dance rhythms that I remembered from my dad's band. The only things I recall, was breaking a plastic head on my snare whilst playing of all things, a waltz! I was paid the princely sum of £2, I think it was just enough for a replacement head.

Anyway I've jumped ahead a couple of weeks; I had still retained contact with John Nockolds who was now playing guitar with King's Lynn band Mike Prior & The Escorts. In mid October I had spoken to him and he told me their drummer Dennis Scott had an offer to join Denny Raven & The Sabres and was probably going to join them. The next week I had gone to see the Escorts play at a cinema in Sutton Bridge, I liked what I saw and chatted to the band, John told them I was good drummer and looking for a band. Nothing was decided that night, but I arranged to meet John one day in the last week of October when he told me Dennis was definitely leaving, so without the band hearing me, no audition, would I like to join the band. Of course I leapt at the chance; my first gig was to be Saturday 3rd November 1962. I had made it! If the band liked me and I liked the band this was the opportunity I had been waiting for.

Chapter three – Mike Prior &The Escorts (November 1962 – April 1963)

In the week leading up to my first gig with Mike Prior & The Escorts on November 3rd, I was both nervous and excited at the prospect of joining my first band. Although it was never discussed I knew those first gigs would be very much a trial period and I had to get it right. I practised constantly and read and re-read the song list John Nockolds had given me.
As I packed my gear into my Austin Devon and made my way to Fakenham on that cold November Saturday, I felt ready to rock 'n' roll and all the nervous apprehension of the week went away.
The Escorts line up when I joined was Mike Prior (lead vocals), John Nockolds (guitar, vocals), Al Drake (guitar, vocals) and Pete Carter (bass, vocals). Unlike many local bands the Escorts had a roadie/driver, John Wickham who drove the band around in an old van. John Wickham was a great guy who remained with the band all the way through.
I was surprised to see quite a few friends there from Dersingham, Ingoldisthorpe and Snettisham who had come to support me. As they mingled with Escorts fans I could hear the occasional comment as to how I would fit in. Dennis Scott was quite a respectable and talented drummer, he had been with the band since they formed in the January of that year and had been playing drums far longer than I had, so it was a hard act to follow.
The set list was a mixture of instrumentals, (The Shadows, Nero & The Gladiators, The Ventures, etc) such as *Apache, Hall Of The Mountain King* and *Walk Don't Run*, together with Chuck Berry, Gene Vincent, Eddie Cochran and Little Richard songs. Conway Twitty was firm favourite, slow smoochy songs included *Only Make Believe* and the instrumental *Sleepwalk*. Mike and the band were also heavily into Screamin' Lord Sutch & The Savages (such notables as Jimmy Page and Ritchie Blackmore passed through the Savages ranks) and the band did a great version of *Jack The Ripper* with Mike in a cloak complete with a false knife and the rest of the band wearing masks, this was a great crowd pleaser. The gear the band had at that time was very primitive, just a couple of WEM and Selmer amps. The PA system was a homemade speaker cabinet (made out of an orange box) with a Leak amp. Al had a Watkins Rapier guitar, John, I think had a Burns guitar and Pete had a Framus bass.
Musically the Escorts were far ahead of their rivals, Al Drake even at an early age could read and arrange music, and as well as being a talented guitarist he also played keyboards, trumpet and violin. Perhaps his greatest asset, he possessed a natural ear and could hear any note, song, chord or whatever and tell you what it was. One of his party pieces was to fart and then proceed to name the note and pick it out on guitar!
John Nockolds had been playing guitar for some time, he was heavily influenced by Hank Marvin and loved all those instrumentals and could interpret them quite well. Pete Carter was another natural musician, everything always seemed easy to Pete and as well as being an outstanding bass player he was a pretty good guitarist too. Mike Prior was just Mike! He was a talented singer, particularly on ballads and was always good at picking out unusual and quirky songs.
We played three sets that night between 8.00 and 11.45 to a responsive audience and the band went down well. I thought I had fitted in quite well and didn't make too many cock ups. I liked them and more importantly they liked me! One or two of the

fans came up and congratulated me on doing a good job, my mind buzzed and I felt a real high as I packed up my drums.

You might wonder how I managed to learn to play all these songs so quickly, with no previous experience in playing in a rock group, after all it had only been three months since I first seriously got behind a drum kit. I had worked hard at developing my technique, but I was also fortunate in having a good listening ear and I usually only have to hear something once to memorise it. Combine this with a good sense of rhythm and timing and being somewhat of a natural drummer, all helped in fine tuning my abilities. Song titles have never meant much to me when playing music. I didn't so much listen to the melody or words, but concentrated on the chord changes, fills etc, and by working closely with the bass line soon learnt where and when to fill in with cymbal accents and drum patterns.

We had a quick chat after packing everything up and I was relieved to hear I had got the job. I knew it would take a little time to get to know everyone properly, but they were a great bunch of guys and I'd been accepted.

The band rehearsed at the old Labour club in Chapel Street King's Lynn, since demolished and now the site of the Borough Council offices. These rehearsals usually took place on a Tuesday or Wednesday evening, my first rehearsal was scheduled for the following Wednesday. Although Al Drake usually arranged the songs, I was pleased to see the entire band had an input in choice of material and interpretation.

We ran through a couple of new songs and I brushed up on some endings to a few more. Our next booking was the following week at a Youth Club in Spalding, playing in a converted Church.

This was very much a transition period for groups, the Beatles and the Liverpool sound had yet to have much impact. Cliff Richard & The Shadows were still popular, but there was a sign that music was moving on, and for once it would be the Brits that made that change happen, although we pinched American songs and their ideas, it would take several more months before those changes bore fruition.

Mike Prior & The Escorts were popular, but were still struggling for gigs, most work was obtained on a gig and the band had yet to learn the art of selling themselves, but this would all change in the months ahead.

We were all scattered about the area, Mike and John were the only band members to live in King's Lynn. Al lived near Long Sutton, Pete was from Shouldham and of course I was from Dersingham. Beside John Wickham I was the only one who could drive and had transport, although Mike had a moped which regularly burst into flames as he rode it around the town!

Bands like the Sabres and the Escorts used to meet up at the Whisky A-Go-Go, or just the Whisky as it became known. The Whisky was a coffee bar on the corner of Broad Street, King's Lynn (long demolished and now roughly where the Westgate store is situated), and a popular haunt for all teenagers throughout the 60's. Al and Pete used to come in by bus, or get a lift and John Wickham picked us up and drove to the gig.

We played at quite a few Youth Clubs in the area, but it was the high profile prestige gigs that we wanted to concentrate on, venues such as Lynford Hall, near Thetford, Corn Exchange King's Lynn, Rollerdrome Cromer, Sunset Rooms Dereham, Gala Norwich and Banham, near Norwich, were just a few of the coveted venues most local bands were after. These gigs usually meant you would be support band to a name act and gave us the opportunity to play to larger audiences outside of our local patch. We were also able to chat to these 'stars' and sometimes use their gear. Other important venues included the Kit Kat Hunstanton, Wreningham, near Norwich,

Attleborough and the RAF bases that had clubs open to civilians, such as Marham and Swanton Morley.

Among the gigs the band appeared at during the last two months of the year were – Lynford Hall November 18th, Kit Kat Hunstanton November 25th, Lynford Hall December 6th, Marcham Hall March December 8th, Kit Kat December 9th, Wreningham December 22nd, Corn Exchange King's Lynn December 24th and Casino Hunstanton December 31st.

1963 arrived with an icy blast from the arctic making it was one of the worst winter's on record. Snow and ice together made travelling difficult right up to early March and with no heater in the van, ice formed on the inside making journeys to gigs an 'unforgettable experience' to say the least. About this time Mike obtained an ancient Morris 10 for I think ten quid, and decided he was going to learn to drive, so occasionally I would ride 'shotgun' with him to a gig. One icy night after volunteering to take Al back to Long Sutton, and only a half mile from my home the car skidded on some black ice and rolled over with all my drums in the back, luckily I was travelling slowly and no major damage was caused either to me or my drums, however Mike's car was a write off with the local garage calling it unsafe to drive in the first place. I don't think Mike ever forgave me for rolling his car and for years after kept reminding me.

All of the bands used to meet up after gigs at 'Jacks' (Jack Barrie) who ran a 'greasy spoon' café and fish and chip shop in Railway Road King's Lynn. Jack's humble abode was a home from home to all musicians. Not just local, but also to the many 'name' bands that played venues in Heacham, Dereham, Norwich and Gt.Yarmouth who broke their journey with a plateful of double sausage, eggs, chips and beans with of course bread and butter to soak up the grease and a mug of tea to wash it all down. 'Jacks' became a legend and some London bands made a detour just to call in at this notorious meeting place. It wasn't just the food, it was a place where bands could swap stories and talk about the latest gear, and on a Friday or Saturday night the place used to be buzzing until Jack threw us out sometimes as late as 4.00am. Some of the bands and musicians I remember that called in at 'Jacks' included Sounds Incorporated, The Tornadoes (of *Telstar* fame), The Barron Knights, Alvin Lee's Jaybirds, Screamin' Lord Sutch and many of the Liverpool bands. Jack Barrie was a musician's friend and had many business interests linked to the music industry. He went on to joint-manage manage The Tea Time Four and later had a hand in launching the careers of 'Boz' Burrell (before he joined Bad Company) and Ian McLagan of the Small Faces. Later on Jack also managed the Marquee Club in London, together with Marquee Artists.

Our 1963 date list was beginning to look healthier with gigs at King's Lynn's Corn Exchange on January 5th, supporting the Flee-Rekker's who's hit at the time was *Green Jeans* (a take off of Greensleeves). Their drummer was Mickey Waller who went on to join Jeff Beck. Other dates we played during those snowy first weeks of the New Year included the Corn Exchange again on January 12th, Kit Kat January 13th, Sunset Rooms Dereham January 19th, Lynford Hall February 2nd, 17th and March 2nd and various other dates at Attleborough, Wreningham, Spalding, Downham Market and King's Lynn.

On joining Mike Prior & The Escorts I soon realised my drum kit was not up to the job, the stands and fittings kept slipping or falling over and to stop the bass drum from disappearing over the edge of the stage, I had to rope it in tying it round my drum stool as an anchor. In January I went to see Mike Langwade who at the time was manager of Wheeler's music shop. Mike or Michael Langwade was later a Mayor of

King's Lynn. He was a good friend to all the local musicians and he stocked or could obtain most of the popular makes of instruments and amps. I ordered a Premier kit in a mahogany finish. I also bought all new Zyldian cymbals to replace the cheap Zyn's. I wasn't too sure how I was going to pay for all this, however I traded all my old gear in, used the small available balance as a deposit and again had to work up the courage to ask my dad to sign the loan agreement, but before I got around to this small matter my new kit duly arrived at the shop. Wheeler's had proudly put my gleaming new kit in their shop front window, that would have been okay, but for one rather obvious sign. In large black lettering stuck on the front of the bass drum for all to see was – supplied to RICKY MEEK of THE ESCORTS. My father caught sight of this before I did and I had rather a lot of explaining to do, he reminded me I didn't have a job and how was I going to pay for my new drums out of just my band earnings. I couldn't tell him that my mum and gran were bailing me out quite regularly. Over the course of the next couple of days I finally got him to agree to sign the new loan agreement, although he wasn't too pleased with my headstrong argument that I was going to 'make it' one day.

By the spring of 1963 we had introduced nearly all new material into the band's set list; the Beatles had really broken through with not just *Love Me Do* but had now released *Please Please Me* which had shot right up the charts. Also other new bands, mainly from Liverpool were also starting to have an impact on the charts. The Searchers, Gerry & The Pacemakers, Freddy & The Dreamers, Dave Berry & The Cruisers, Billy J Kramer & The Dakotas and The Big Three were just some of the new names that were really changing the music scene. Bands were now appearing on stage in collarless Beatle jackets, with high Cuban heel boots and growing their hair longer.

So, just as music was changing so Mike Prior & The Escorts was to change, we jointly decided to reluctantly part company with John Nockolds. John had been in the band from the beginning, but we didn't see the need of a two guitar line up with the new music we wanted to play, we amicably said goodbye to John, got new stage gear, had some publicity photos taken, business cards printed and actively went out and sold the band.

Within weeks we would be playing more and more high profile gigs as support to a number of name bands and would become friends with several famous musicians, including Alvin Lee of Ten Years After fame. We would get the chance to appear on TV – and to put our trust in a Manager!

Chapter Four – Mixing Paint With Pasadena! (April 1963 – November 1963)

In early April I parted company with my faithful Austin Devon, the head gasket had blown and it just wasn't worth spending any more money, money I didn't have, to keep the car on the road. I looked round and found a 1955 Austin A50, not brilliant, but at least roadworthy, my gran lent me the £100 I needed and I was back on the road once more.

Although the gigs were coming in, money or lack of it was becoming a serious problem. I was spending far more than what came in, it didn't need a mathematical genius to work out I had to remedy this and fast! Against my better judgement I decided to look round for a day job. I saw a vacancy in the local paper for a general assistant at James Lambert (Ironmongers & Builders Merchants), a kind of a pre B&Q that sold to the trade, as well as the general public. Although a Snettisham company this vacancy was for their Hunstanton branch. I phoned up and got an interview, the manager was Reg Brown, it turned out he knew my dad, so we got on quite well from the start. He offered me the job there and then at £6.00 per week, not much you may think, but in 1963 this wasn't a bad wage and it meant I could keep out of debt and keep my dad happy in one foul swoop!

I started work in early May, and soon got the hang of mixing paint and learning all there was to know about door handles and garden furniture. I had to work all day on Saturdays which was a real downer. I was usually out with the band on most Friday and Saturday nights, so having to get out of bed in time for an 8.30am start on a Saturday morning was no joke as time would tell.

The Escorts were slowly making a name for themselves, and in the months ahead we would have the opportunity to play alongside many of the top recording bands. Alan Lockwood, a former drummer with the Sabres started promoting dances around the area, at such venues as King's Lynn Corn Exchange and Banham. He would bring Alvin Lee's Jaybirds down from Nottingham for a three night booking. They would play the Maids Head in King's Lynn on Thursday, perhaps the Corn Exchange on Friday and Banham on the Saturday, and we would play as support act on the Friday and Saturday. Alvin Lee of course went on to fame and international success with Ten Years After, but in 1963 he was just another musician in a band trying to make it big time. We worked with Alvin several times over the coming months and got to know him and the band quite well, he was a brilliant guitarist and we knew one day he would achieve the success he deserved.

Other bands Lockwood booked that we would get to work with, included Screamin' Lord Sutch, Dave Berry & The Cruisers, Freddy & The Dreamers, The Barron Knights and Sounds Incorporated to name a few. We also nearly got to play alongside the Beatles; this 'nearly' gig was a real disappointment. Alan Lockwood had a contract signed for the Beatles to appear at King's Lynn Corn Exchange, with a 'get out' clause. If their latest single got into the top three in the charts the price of the band would go up considerably, and he would have the option to cancel. Of course just about every single went to number one and Lockwood cancelled the gig. I think he always regretted his decision, and I believe he still has that contract! It would have been a great coup to have the 'fab four' play King's Lynn, and an even greater one for Mike Prior & The Escorts to appear on the same bill, unfortunately it was not to be.

Alan Lockwood also promoted some local dances at venues such as North Lynn Community Centre, East Winch Village Hall and the Town Hall, Downham Market.

He would book two local bands for a shared billing, of course every band wanted to play the final set, as this would seem as though they were the 'headliner' band. We often played alongside our friendly rivals such as Danny Eves & The Strollers. I knew them well, as I had worked with the band back in March on two or three occasions when their drummer Nigel Raines couldn't make it for one reason or another. They were a good band and would come out of retirement many years later to prove it once more. Other bands included old friends Danny Ford & The Offbeats and the newly formed Tea Time Four. The Tea Time Four were always different; their front men were two very competent musicians from the Spalding area, Barry 'Fats' Dean and Boz Burrell. Both were excellent singers and guitarists who so impressed the landlord of the Maids Head, Colin Atkinson, that he began to manage the band, he eventually set up a joint management company with Jack Barrie that handled the bands bookings. Fats and Boz both changed to playing bass, and went on to greater things! But more of that later. Another band we shared the stage with was Denny Raven & The Sabres, led by the 'oldest teenager in town' Tony Relph. He earned this title because he was some nine or ten years older than the rest of the band, although you wouldn't think it. He was a real charmer and Londoner by birth, he had the good looks that soon had all the girls falling over themselves to get to the front of the stage. But Tony had to share the spotlight with lead vocalist Denny Raven, aka Barry Leader, who also had the looks and personality. Little did I know I would be joining the Sabres in the months ahead?

Although I was handling most of our bookings, Alan Lockwood wanted to become our manager; he was a smooth talker and as an agent, he knew a lot of people in the music business and promoted his own dances, which in theory meant we should never run out of gigs. After lengthy discussions we decided to go along with him, we wanted to go further with the band and promises of work in London, Birmingham and Nottingham with more money, and perhaps the chance of a recording contract sealed our fate!

I had written to Anglia TV in late spring to try and get the band a spot on TV. They were not too keen on local bands, but Paul Chris had appeared a couple of times, so I thought we might be in with a chance. I didn't hear back straight away so I asked Mike Langwade to write in with support for us, telling Anglia what a great band we were. Sometime in late June I had a phone call at work from Peter Fenn, who was musical director at Anglia, inviting the band for an audition for a new TV show called 'Junior Angle Club'. It was a kind of 'Blue Peter' for teenagers. Sandy Sandford was the host and the show was scheduled to be recorded on Mondays, going out the following Friday teatime. We jumped at the this opportunity and within a couple of weeks rolled into the Anglia TV studios in Norwich on a Saturday morning ready to impress Peter Fenn. Mike had recently learned the Temperance 7's surprise hit, *Home In Pasadena*. It was really a trad jazz number, but we had adapted it, and it always went down well. So instead of rocking out, Mike just sat on Pete's speaker cabinet and in a very relaxed manner sang the song, even jumping down and performing a little dance during the solo. Peter Fenn must have been pretty impressed, because he offered us a spot on 'Junior Angle Club' straight away, without us playing any other song. An appearance on TV back in 1963 was the real deal! We would record the programme on Monday 29th July, and it would be broadcast on Friday 2nd August.

Of course I had to take the Saturday off from work for the audition which wasn't a problem with Reg Brown, but I think some members of staff thought I received preferential treatment, as I rarely arrived into work on time, and left sometimes early to get to a gig. Looking back I was fortunate to have such an understanding boss and I suppose I really did take advantage of this fact, but Reg was interested in my musical career, and didn't mind when people use to call into the shop to see me for booking the band, and he even got us some gigs!

We nearly didn't appear on 'Junior Angle Club', originally the band were only going to be paid reasonable expenses, but Alan Lockwood as our Manager, insisted we get paid the same as any TV appearance. Anglia declined at first and threatened to cancel our appearance, in the end we all had to join the Musician's Union and Anglia agreed to pay us union rates for our TV debut.

July was a busy month for the band, besides the TV show to look forward to we had eleven gigs to play, including support band to rock n' roll star Gene Vincent. Vincent was still a very big name in 1963, and had gone through a resurgence of his career after his involvement with the car crash that had claimed the life of his friend Eddie Cochran. On tour in the UK, he was being backed by the Outlaws, which at that time included no other than guitarist Ritchie Blackmore, bassist Chas Hodges and drummer Mick Underwood, all would achieve international fame in the years ahead. (Blackmore with Deep Purple, Hodges with Chas & Dave and Underwood with Gillan and Peter Frampton) Vincent was booked to appear at King's Lynn Corn Exchange, this was very much a prestige local gig for the band and the Corn Exchange quickly sold out. In those days it was a huge echoing barn of a place, not the plush concert hall of today, but many an international star packed out the King's Lynn venue in the 60's.

40 years down the road I can still remember this night well. Vincent had lost none of his powers as a performer, dressed in black and despite his injured leg, he was mesmerizing to watch, as he performed all those 50's hits including, *Say Mama* and of course *Be-Bop-A-Lula*. Vincent was a rock 'n' roll hero and one of the founders of pop and rock music we know and love today. Off stage Vincent was a different character altogether, very moody, in fact a strange guy, who became more revealing the longer we chatted to him after the gig. He told us he no longer wanted to tour, and his managers were making him do all these one-nighters, (the previous night he had been in Wales) and he just wanted out. He had a liking for firearms and always carried a gun with him, which he proudly showed us. He also had wife trouble and said he intended to shoot her, and sure enough sometime after our meeting he did threaten his wife with a gun and was arrested!

Other appearances in the month included another at the Corn Exchange with the Eagles (no! – not the American band, but the successful Bristol band that notched up a few hits), plus Banham, Cromer, Lowestoft, Lynford Hall, RAF Marham.and a few smaller venues round the Norfolk coast.

July 29th came round very quickly. As we headed to Anglia TV studios on that bright sunny morning I think we all felt we would be making it big time! Nothing could stop us! Nothing can replace the dreams of youth. We had to be at the studio by 9.30am, ready to set up our gear. All the amps and PA had to be checked and set up by the Anglia studio technicians, and my drum kit was placed on a small platform just off centre. Mikes were then placed, to pick up from the amps and PA, with four additional mikes picking up my drums and cymbals. Then everything was fed into Anglia's sound mixer, and there were monitors for the band to hear what was going on. The studio was all decked out ready for the performance with producer Paul Johnson directing everyone, so we knew the running order of the programme. Mike Prior & The Escorts was to perform two songs of our choice, none to run over four minutes. We would play one song about half way through, and the second would play out the programme. The morning was spent rehearsing the running order and getting the sound balance right for the band. Besides the Escorts, presenter Sandy Sandford did a couple of spots, and there were one or two other guests, including 'Romper Room' presenter Miss Roselyn, how many remember her?

After lunch at the studios we all had to go through make up, (and it was in the good old days of black and white TV) then run through the show once, take a short break, and then producer Paul Johnson made his final checks. After this, there were no room for errors and the show was for real, and recorded. We never had time to feel nervous; we just got on and played! The two songs we picked out were the Big Three's *Some Other Guy* and we played out on the Beatles *Twist & Shout*, which had rocketed to the top of the charts. There was no time to see our results, as we had to be out of the studio in time for the evening news. Seeing Mike Prior & The Escorts name printed in the TV Times, as special guest band on 'Junior Angle Club' was really something, and we couldn't wait to see our results when the show was aired on the following Friday.

I never had time to drive home after work to see the broadcast, so a couple at work who lived in Hunstanton invited me round to watch the show. I thought we played really well and the sound balance was good, it was fascinating to watch, and it would be the only occasion I would have to watch myself on TV. (other TV appearances were always live) I would love to have the opportunity to view it today, but this was long before video recording. Most pre-recorded TV was done on huge sound/vision recorders, and the tapes would be wiped clean and then re-used. However the father of a girlfriend took some photographs straight off the TV screen, and I eagerly looked forward to seeing these. Unfortunately we split up in the meantime, so I thought I would never get to see them, but a few weeks later she did send the photos to me, they came out well as you can judge for yourself (they are re-produced for this book).

We played Brancaster Village Hall on the night of the broadcast and there were an amazing amount of people there, and we spent our breaks signing autographs, we really felt like stars!

August again was a busy month with thirteen gigs, that included two appearances at RAF Marham, Banham (with the Barron Knights), Cromer (with Screamin' Lord Sutch), and Norwich (with the Eagles), then on to Lowestoft the next day to play two shows at a theatre with Keith Powell & The Valets, and Peter Jay & The Jaywalkers. Peter Jay was probably the first British rock 'n' roll drummer to put real showmanship into his own solo spot; he used a sequence of lights which flashed on and off, as he struck each drum. This was quite impressive with the stage lights turned down. A sitting down audience was new to us but we went down well, and all had a great time.

We were working further from our local area and September saw us at Gorleston Floral Hall, Chatteris, Norwich and a show at Great Yarmouth, but we managed to fit in local gigs at the Maids Head and Corn Exchange.

On October 3rd Alan Lockwood fixed us up with a national talent spotting audition being held at the Queens Hall, Leeds. There were going to be a lot of bands there trying to get just that one lucky break, to be seen by a record producer and a top agent, to give just that final push to the top. I managed to get the day off work, as we had to be in Leeds by early afternoon to be told the running order and format. Each band could play two songs; I think we did the Beatles *Thank You Girl* and our version of *Hog For You*. Setting up time was helped by having a huge stage with plenty of room for all the bands to set up, play and pack up. There was also a show band booked to play in a few intervals during the evening. The place was packed with people and the only other band there, which I remember was the Grumbleweeds. At one point Al Drake got up to play piano with the show band, when their regular pianist fell ill and couldn't play. It was a memorable evening, but a disappointing one, as we failed to make an impression on the judges and came home feeling slightly rejected. We didn't get paid expenses and with taking a day's unpaid leave, an expensive one, but we put it all down to experience, you win some, you lose some! We didn't get back to King's Lynn until 6.00am and I was exhausted and took another day off work, this time Reg was not happy with my non-appearance at 8.30am.

On October 20th we played Cromer Rollerdrome with the Paramounts. This was my first meeting with drummer B J (Barrie) Wilson and keyboard player Garry Brooker. Guitarist Robin Trower was also in the band. Of course all three would eventually form one of the UK's most innovative bands Procol Harum. The Paramounts were from Southend and had charted with their version of *Love Potion No 9*. Barrie and I would meet up again in the mid '70's and he became one of my closest friends.

As November rolled around, little did I know the changes that would happen before the end of the month? The band had bookings for Lynn's Corn Exchange and Maids Head, as well as Banham, with the Jaybirds on November 9th. On Thursday November 14th we were working on the North Norfolk coast at Thornham. As the band had to pass through Dersingham they picked me up, and dropped me off on the way back. We arranged a time to meet for the gig the following evening, but that night at Thornham would be the very last time I played with Mike Prior & The Escorts.

The next morning I had a phone call at work from Tony Relph of the Sabres, telling me that Alan Lockwood had persuaded Dennis Scott to re-join the Escorts, from that evening, and would I like to join the Sabres. I was stunned by this news, as I had had no indication that this was about to happen. Other than a couple of minor disagreements with Alan Lockwood over certain band policies, everything else with the band appeared normal.

I quickly thought things over and agreed to join the Sabres, my first gig was that night at Littleport with just one small problem – I didn't have a drum kit, it was still with the Escorts!

Chapter Five – Can It Really Be Hamburg? (November 1963 – January 1964)

I had little time to think about my sudden and unexpected departure from the Escorts. We had all worked so hard to push the band into the spotlight, and I thought almost to the brink of 'making it'. In those first couple of hours following the phone call from Tony Relph I felt angry and bitterly disappointed at what had happened, but at the same time realised I had to look ahead, and Denny Raven & The Sabres were West Norfolk's top group and opportunity to join them a positive move to advance my musical career and get somewhere.

So by the time I met up with the Sabres at the Whisky later that November evening, I tried to put all thoughts of the Escorts behind me. Of course I knew all the guys in the band quite well from countless times, sharing gigs together and hanging out at the Whiskey and Jack Barrie's. The band's line up was lead vocals Denny Raven, aka Barry Leader, guitar /vocals Tony Relph, guitar/vocals Maurice 'Mo' Pegg and bass/vocals Dave Stoddard. The Sabres were a different band from the Escorts; they had a very good stage routine complete with uniform dance steps and identical white Fender guitars.

As I sat down with them to talk about the band's set list, I suddenly thought 'where's my drum kit, what am I going to do with no drums?' I quickly mentioned this fact to Tony, who told me not to worry, I could use Dennis's kit in the meantime, and he would get the drum kits changed over. But it would be a couple of weeks before I finally got my drums returned.

My first appearance with the Sabres was at Littleport on Friday 15th November, followed the next night by the Gala, Norwich with Russ Sainty & The Nu-Notes, which featured guitarist Roger Dean who would later join blues man John Mayall. I quickly realised the band had quite a following, this was something new. Although the Escorts always had fans and the band usually went down well, with the Sabres fans travelled to see the band from all over East Anglia, there were a lot more girls who stood at the front of the stage and screamed – I thought 'I'm going to enjoy this'. The set list was different from the Escorts and included early soul-type songs, which Denny Raven could interpret with ease; he was also a very good ballad singer with Mo, Tony and Dave singing back up harmonies.

Other gigs in November included USAF Mildenhall (20th), Blackfriars Hall King's Lynn (22nd), a significant date it was the day John F Kennedy was assassinated. RAF Feltwell (23rd), Attleborough (27th), Newmarket (28th) and a shared billing with the Tea Time Four at East Winch (30th)

Like every musician in groups playing up and down the country in 1963, I wanted to get to Hamburg, and little did I know on joining the Sabres my dreams were about to become a reality and my sacking from the Escorts was the best thing that could have happened to me. In late November we spotted an advert in the 'Melody Maker' seeking bands to work at The Top Ten Club in Hamburg, they would be holding auditions in early December at the Gaumont Theatre in Ipswich. Tony quickly phoned the number to find out more and hopefully get an audition.

By the end of 1963, Beatlemania had swept over most of Europe, and Hamburg, European Capital of rock n' roll was clamouring for more English bands. Bands from England had been playing the smaller clubs like the Kaiserkeller since the early '60's; but it wasn't until the Beatles hit it big that the larger and more famous clubs like the Star Club and The Top Ten Club, began searching hard for new bands to satisfy the music hungry kids of Hamburg. It was at the Top Ten that the Beatles had their early success and had really broken through, after working the smaller clubs around Hamburg's legendary St Pauli nightspots. Also making a name for himself was a certain ex-Norwich musician named Tony Sheridan.

Initially both the Star and Top Ten Clubs were recruiting bands from the Liverpool area, but by the end of 1963 bands from London and Glasgow were now a familiar sight on the Hamburg music scene.

There were quite a number of talented German, Dutch, Swedish and French bands around, but they all seemed to share a common problem! A general lack of the English language to make much sense of the lyrics, plus most had a tempo problem, which made a lot of these bands sound like a runaway train! This is why the Star and Top Ten rarely employed non English speaking bands.

The Top Ten Club was located in the St Pauli district, Hamburg's red light area, right on the notorious Reeperbahn. Owned and managed by a young music enthusiast named Peter Eckhorn. It was a large club and was formally a music hall owned by Peter's father.

In early 1963 Peter Eckhorn began looking further afield than Liverpool for bands to play his music venue. Firstly Peter employed a resident sax player named Rikki Barnes, who had come to Hamburg with a talented Scottish band called the Bobby Patrick Big Six. With Barnes's help, several great bands from Glasgow began appearing at the Top Ten, one of these bands had a young girl singer named Isabelle Bond, who soon became the resident girl singer at the Top Ten, but still more English bands were needed.

Iain Hines had originally been enticed to Hamburg with the Jets to work at Bruno Koschmider's club the Kaiserkeller. Hines was a talented keyboard player; he had backed early '60's stars Tommy Bruce and Ricky Valance. His brother is the actor Fraser Hines, who rose to fame appearing in 'Dr Who' and 'Emmerdale' .Hines returned to England after a while, but the lure of Hamburg proved too much and he soon returned looking for work. In due course he began working at the Top Ten. He got on well with Peter Eckhorn, and it wasn't long before Eckhorn offered him the job of musical director and talent scout for the club. Hines soon headed back once again to England to search out new bands for the Top Ten.

Denny Raven & The Sabres was lucky and got an audition in early December. We duly drove down to Ipswich, hopeful of impressing Iain Hines and landing a month long contract at the famous club. There were many bands from all over the UK, so we realised we had some tough competition. Looking back it all seemed quite easy, we played three or four varied songs from our set list, making sure we injected the same enthusiasm and showmanship as a regular gig, but out of the dozen's of bands who tried for an audition, only a handful were successful, and none of these were local, other than the Sabres. Iain liked the band and the show we put on and we were offered a month long contract starting February 1964, with more work to follow, if we went down well with the German audience. This took a little while to sink in, it really was our dream come true, we were riding the clouds and I thought to myself,' talk about being in the right place at the right time'. The Sabres would be the first East Anglian band to work in Hamburg.

After getting an audition, my old band mates in the Escorts unfortunately failed to make any impression. On the day they suffered from technical difficulties and had to finish their set early and did not make it through the audition.

The band had a lot to organise, but for now we had to complete our December bookings, sixteen in total. We had already played Cromer with Eden Kane & The

Downbeats and still had gigs at Lynn's Maids Head, Ally Club Cambridge, Newmarket, Gorleston, USAF Mildenhall, USAF Sculthorpe, Wells, Alysham, Lynn's Corn Exchange on Boxing Day and Heacham on New Years Eve.

Besides the momentous news on the forthcoming Hamburg trip, the other news was that I had changed my car. The Austin A50 had served me well, but I had to get something more up to date. I'd seen a 1962 Hillman Husky for sale at a local garage in Hunstanton, the Husky was an early version of an estate car. I could put the back seat down flat, so when I did have my drums home it would be a lot easier loading. With the deal done and only a small loan to take out I entered 1964 with renewed hope and felt the New Year could only bring me fame and fortune!

The first problem that occurred was Dave Stoddard would not be able to come to Hamburg with us, which was a real blow. His bosses had flatly refused to give him any time off, paid or unpaid. The rest of us were luckier, we had all managed to get the month off. Tony spoke with Pete Carter and offered him the job, and it took Pete all of two seconds to accept. Pete would officially be joining us towards the end of January when Dave would quit the band.

The Escorts were on the verge of splitting up and by the end of the month Mike Prior had left to join the Tea Time Four. Al Drake and Dennis Scott did continue for a short while, replacing Pete with Bernie Barton on bass. They went to France in February, but while playing at a US airbase, Dennis was struck down with appendicitis and they had to return home.

In 1964 there was no free and easy access to European Countries, particularly to work. We had to get passports, then on to the German Embassy in London to apply for visas and work permits. The Embassy required proof of work, our contracts had yet to arrive, so it meant further trips to London during the month to iron out the final details.

We had bookings to fulfil in the run up to our departure to Hamburg, but of course we had to cancel all our UK work for the month of February. Most of the venues were sympathetic and understood why we had to cancel, but equally some failed to appreciate why we wouldn't be appearing.

The final week before leaving for Germany was hectic with Tony finalising our ferry crossing from Harwich to Hook Of Holland, for Friday 31st January. The media were getting excited; this was a big news story in our part of the world. There were press interviews and photos. Tony Scase from the BBC turned up with a TV crew to film us getting ready, packing our gear into the band trailer and also to record the band to use as a soundtrack for the film. The BBC put this out on the Friday evening as we made our way through Holland!

My parents had mixed feelings about me going to Hamburg, they knew this was something I wanted to do and no way would I miss this opportunity, but wondered what I would get up to. My workmates were quite supportive and Reg Brown and John Lambert were brilliant in giving me the time off. I'd become somewhat a local celebrity in the shop, with customers calling in to wish me luck. I felt like some intrepid explorer about to embark on a journey to the upper reaches of the Amazon!

With all my bags packed and my drums already loaded in the band trailer, my dad took me into King's Lynn, picking up 'Mo'Pegg on route to meet up with the rest of guys for a 6.30am getaway to board the Hook Of Holland ferry, leaving Harwich in the late morning - and so our Hamburg adventure began!

Chapter Six – Hamburg Days (February 1964)

It seemed a long journey down to Harwich on that chilly winter's day. In 1964 there was little in the way of dual carriageways, just winding twisty roads that seemed to go on forever. When we eventually arrived at the Port of Harwich we were subject to a thorough search by Customs to make sure we weren't smuggling anything illegal abroad, and at last cleared to board the ferry. The ferries that crossed the North Sea daily were not the modern roll on, roll off of today. All vehicles had to be hoisted aboard by crane, and as the time came for Tony's Zephyr and the band's trailer to be lifted aboard, we all stood anxiously looking up and trusting nothing would break and send all our gear crashing onto the dockside. Thankfully everything was loaded without a hitch and we left England late morning for the six hour crossing.
By the time we arrived at the Hook of Holland it was dark, cold and raining heavily. We again had long delays with unloading and customs formalities to contend with, and it was well after 8.00pm by the time we were able to hit the road for our long overnight journey through Holland and into Germany travelling north to Hamburg, a long road trip.
Tony had mapped the route out quite well, but as we left the 'Hook' instead of travelling towards Amsterdam we found we were on the outskirts of Rotterdam instead. After a quick turnaround we managed to find the right autobahn and made our way north through Utrecht and on to Arnhem where we found a friendly tavern for a pit stop to refuel with the finest Dutch steak and chips. Sometime in the early hours of Saturday we were at the German border, the German Customs made us unload the trailer for a complete search, and then they checked all the passports, visas and work permits before we were finally allowed into Germany. Once more on the road again we managed to find a bar still open somewhere near Osnabruck and made a brief stop for a beer, then onwards hoping we would be in Hamburg sometime mid morning in time to unload, get to know everyone and grab a few hours kip before we launched ourselves on the Top Ten audience, but as the saying goes 'all good plans don't always pan out'!
While making good progress on the autobahn near Bremen we had a 'blow out' on the nearside trailer tyre, we managed to stop okay and surveyed the damage. The tyre was completely shredded and with no spare we were up 'shit creek without a paddle'. While we pondered on the next move a police patrol car drew alongside, quickly assessing our predicament they offered to escort us to the nearest garage. The trailer was jacked up and the wheel removed and taken to the garage and a new tyre fitted. This delay, cost us over four hours of time and the sleep we so badly needed, but thanks to the German police at least we didn't arrive late.
Hamburg even in 1964 was still re-building after the extensive bomb damage of the 1939-45 war, there were huge areas of un-cleared land and new buildings being put up all around. The Reeperbahn was close to the huge Hamburg port on the River Elbe, which brought ships in from all over the world. The Reeperbahn area had grown up alongside the flourishing port providing it's sailors with every imaginary entertainment that could be invented. Of course the 'oldest game known to man' was well catered for and the 'ladies of the night' were perhaps the first entertainment the Reeperbahn provided, but over the years seedy bars arrived with its transvestites and S & M trade. There were naked girls wrestling in mud, lap dancers and live sex shows. Music clubs came late to Hamburg, but to the thousands of merchant seaman

passing through the Port of Hamburg, besides the lure of girls and booze, music was also high on the list of desires and with the boom of rock n' roll, music venues sprang up like mushrooms. With the help of the Beatles fame two clubs would really be successful, and The Top Ten and the Star Club soon became known worldwide.

On arrival at the Top Ten in the late afternoon, we were greeted by Iain Hines and club owner Peter Eckhorn, who showed us around. For the first night we would be staying at a hotel just down the street. After nearly 36 hours travelling without sleep, we were knackered to say the least, but there was no time to even think about it!

We soon got into the Hamburg lifestyle pretty quickly, we had to or we would have never survived past the first week. Iain knew this and produced these 'magic pills'. Amphetamine tablets like preludin or 'prels' as they were known, had been around years before the Reeperbahn crowd discovered that taken in sufficient quantity they could keep you awake and on a high for days at a time, if you added alcohol into the equation you had a 'heavy mix'. We gulped our pills down and got on with sorting out our gear. The club provided all the amps, top of the line stuff, Fender twin and bassman amps and a fabulous PA system. All drummers brought their own kit, but to save time these were rotated on a weekly basis as the club always had two bands at any one time, sometimes three, we would use each other's kits just quickly changing any cymbals, stools etc if needed.

The Top Ten was open 7 days a week. Weekdays 7.00pm to 3.00am, Saturday 7.00pm to 6.00am, Sunday 5.00pm to 3.00am, and was always crammed full. We worked one hour on/one hour off, with no days off. Some sets were augmented with the house regulars, Iain Hines (Hammond B3), Rikki Barnes (saxes) and Issy Bond (vocals), and within the first two or three days we had worked out a set list and rehearsed some new material with them.

The other band was the Beatmen from Nottingham, who had been at the club since January 1st, they were a great bunch of guys and made sure we knew the 'ins and outs' of working at the Top Ten, and living on the Reeperbahn.

I shall never forget that opening night, the club was packed tight and the atmosphere was electric, mind blowing in fact with one of the best sound systems I have ever heard, even by today's standards. Our time slot was 8.00pm, which meant we had to go through till 6.00am, as this was a Saturday. The dance floor was always full and we soon got to know what the crowd wanted. The band played our usual sets mixing rock 'n' roll, soul and blues, and even on that first night we drew a regular fan base. With our prels and beer we could have played forever and even as 6.00am loomed the Top Ten was still 'rockin' with just as many people packed into the club as earlier. Nothing could have prepared us for this, it was as if we were living in a dream and someone would eventually tap us on the shoulder and say 'wake up mate, you didn't really think it would be like this!' but it was.

One of the downside of popping these little pills was the inability to get to sleep and even after more than 48 hours we were still not tired. We grabbed some food out of the local 'automat'; this was something new, a machine that dispensed all kinds of goodies, from chocolate bars to a complete meal. Germany was certainly far ahead of England back in 1964.

In the end we did manage to get some three hours sleep, which really set the pattern for all our Hamburg visits, and we kinda' got used to it. We moved out of the hotel and settled in to our accommodation quarters over the Top Ten. The bands living area were three or four dormitory style rooms, with just single and bunk beds situated on two floors, with toilets and a hand basin on another floor, no showers or bath and with little in the way of heating it wasn't always home from home. The Eckhorn family also had self- contained flats within the building, one for Peter, his wife and dog! The other two housed Peter's father, and also Uncle Gushi, who was quite a character!

The beds were the same ones the Beatles had slept in, and the same sheets by the smell of them, but we didn't care we were having a ball. John Lennon's distinctive graffiti was everywhere, on the walls of the washroom and behind doors the little drawings would seem to pop out at you, I even found one on the wall behind my bed! Peter Eckhorn was a good friend to us and made sure we were all 'streetwise'.

The Reeperbahn was a surreal place to live and to five young musicians from the rural countryside, at first quite unnerving and frightening, but never less than exciting! We soon got used to the almost daily fights, fights between the visiting seaman and the locals, fights between local gangs, fights between rival pimps, the usual fights over women. Usually the doorman/bouncer of the various clubs and bars (dressed in their heavy overcoats and caps, complete with heavy gold braid) would deal with the problem. Sometimes matters got out of control, and then the police would arrive armed with teargas and batons to put a stop to any trouble. The doormen were good friends of the visiting bands, and generally looked after us and helped avoid any potential problems of life on the Reeperbahn.

Occasionally, fights would spill into the Top Ten and teargas would be fired while we worked. Many a night we have played a set with stinging eyes and tears streaming down our faces. Firearms were a more frightening experience. I well remember one afternoon a drunken employee holding a bunch of us hostage with a gun, firing an odd bullet into the wall, until someone talked him out of any further damage.

One of the favourite pastimes of the visiting musicians was a trip down the Herbertstrasse. A small blocked off street, almost quaint looking, but when you walked through the small opening of the street all your teenage fantasies were thrust on you 'larger than life'. In large shop size windows sat the available girls in every shape and appearance, sex for sale 24 hours a day, girls clad in leather, girls wrapped in just PVC, girls flicking whips, girls in beautiful underwear, it was all here for the asking (and paying). I suppose it was a stroll through a fantasy supermarket, and as we took our regular walks along the street the girls would call out 'eh eh Beatles, we do special price', but please don't ask if any of us took advantage of this generous offer!

The drug scene was rife, and the many bars were open day and night. All of this was a real culture shock for most bands visiting Hamburg for the first time, who could hardly dream up such happenings, let alone be dropped right in the middle of it. The non-stop partying after the clubs closed, the endless supply of pills washed down with liberal quantities of alcohol took a toll on some band members, but those who survived had the time of their lives and like Tony Sheridan never wanted to go home. I remember a crowd of us being taken by Iain Hines and Tony Sheridan to a bar nicknamed 'the hole', where they were urging us on to chat up two or three 'beautiful girls' sitting at the bar. They had an air of glamour about them, with make-up, nails and clothes just so, only learning later that these 'girls' were really 'boys'.

We soon found out where to eat, there were really only three choices near by, next to the Top Ten was the Steak House, which served steak, chicken with chips and was a regular stop for many. The Seamen's Mission was a short stroll to the port, a lot of musicians visited this homely establishment that served a real 'English breakfast' and welcomed us at anytime, but probably the most popular of eating establishments was the Mambo Shanke, situated just round the corner from the club. This is where all the bands gathered to gossip, get known and generally hang out. We got to know a lot of bands and musicians, including The Checkmates, Rory Storm and former Beatle Pete

Best (dubbed at the time 'the unluckiest man in the world'). The Searchers used to pop in and chat, they were appearing at the Star Club with resident band King Size Taylor & The Dominoes.

The guy at the Mambo use to do his best to satisfy our hunger, but the German bratwursts were not quite the same as the sausages back home! The Mambo also provided another John Lennon memento, in the toilet were a number of drawings and under one distinctive Lennon scrawl was some message written in an almost upside down position, so if you were sitting, you had to raise up to read it, and I shall never forget what was written, 'you are now shitting at an angle of 45degrees' perhaps pure musicians humour, but nevertheless, very funny!

If we got up in time, the afternoons were spent exploring the city, gaining a little culture and trying to learn the language. There were large stores like Karstadt which had a great cake shop, where Phil, the drummer in the Beatmen and I would occasionally pass the time. There was also a huge music store and the guy who ran the drum department use to come to the club several evenings a week and try to persuade me to swap my kit for a Trixon (which was the leading German drum manufacturer).

Because of no bath or shower facilities at the club, we had to use the rather grand and Victorian looking public bathhouse, where matronly looking ladies would provide soap, shampoo and towels for the many bathrooms, which were always immaculate and sparkling clean, and it was the only time we could really feel fresh.

In the Top Ten there was a little old lady who looked after the washrooms, (she was a great favourite of the Beatles, and is mentioned in several books about the band) customers would have to pay her to use the washroom; she also sold chocolate and pep pills! A strange combination I know, she was kind, funny and loved by everybody.

All too soon our month long contract came to an end, we had made many, many friends and the band had been a success, and after all those days of non-stop playing we were a really tight unit. Peter offered us another five weeks starting July 1st, with more money, this was brilliant news and I couldn't wait to get back. We played an extra night on March 1st and reluctantly packed up our gear. I decided to fly back to London. I've always enjoyed flying and liked the idea of arriving home in style!

We had several things planned on our return, the BBC wanted us to go to the Norwich studio and do a live interview and play a couple of numbers, we had press interviews to fit in, and of course we all had to return to our day jobs which none of us really wanted to do after such an exciting month!

The rest of the band didn't entirely have a trouble free journey home, when they had a little accident, just outside of Ipswich!

Rick aged 4

Gran My No.1 Fan!

"Power of Arrest"
Dad's Deputy Marshal Badge

Dad's Band - The Snettisham Hill Billy Band 1950's
L to R Dougie Mears, Noel Linge, Eric Meek and Bertha Thrower

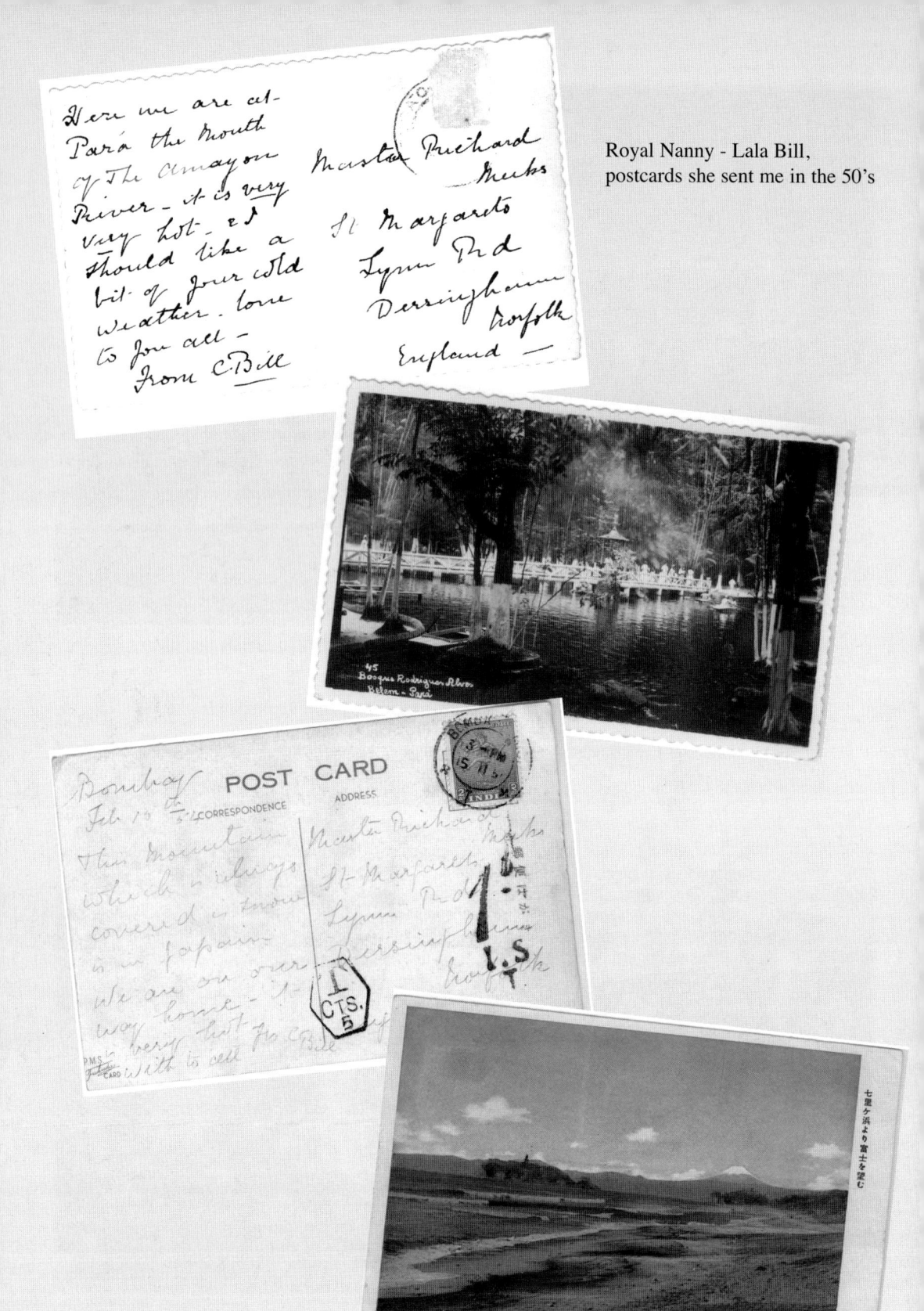

Royal Nanny - Lala Bill,
postcards she sent me in the 50's

Mike Prior & 'The Escorts' - 1963
Mike Prior (vocals), Al Drake (guitar), Pete Carter (bass)
Rick Meek (drums)

Mike Prior & 'The Escorts' - 1963
Mike Prior (vocals), Al Drake (guitar), Pete Carter (bass)
Rick Meek (drums)

Mike Prior & The Escorts appearing on Anglia ITV
Junior Angle Club - August 1963

Denny Raven & The Sabres
at the 'Top Ten Club' Hamburg February 1964
Denny Raven, Tony Relph, Maurice 'Mo' Pegg, Pete Carter & Rick Meek

Passport - Not easy working in
Germany in the 60's
all those work permits, visas
and 'Red Tape'

Denny Raven & The Sabres
at the 'Top Ten Club' Hamburg February 1964
Denny Raven, Tony Relph, Maurice 'Mo' Pegg,
Pete Carter & Rick Meek

Back from Hamburg - March 1964
L to R Tony Relph, Pete Carter, Denny Raven, Rick Meek & Mo Pegg

'Top Ten Club'
Reeperbahn Hamburg 1964

The Sabres group go to Hamburg

THE Sabres, one of West Norfolk's top "beat" groups are to play in the Top Ten Club in Hamburg, Germany.

The Sabres left Lynn early today to begin a month's residency in Hamburg — at the club where The Beatles began their climb to fame.

The Sabres' leader, Tony Relph (30), of 1 Rose Villa, Westgate Street, Shouldham, explained that they had an audition at Ipswich with 15 other groups from the area and they were chosen for the booking.

If they made a success of this first month they could be asked to stay another month. They would then return to West Norfolk and consider turning professional.

THEIR RECORDS

This could be their breakthrough to stardom as the Hamburg club also run their own record company and The Sabres will be recording records for release in Germany.

Tony Relph said that the Top Ten Club were the second biggest in Germany. "They begin at 7 p.m. and go on till 2 a.m. We shall be playing one hour on and two hours off," he said.

One group member, Linda Holden, a vocalist, is unable to join The Sabres for this trip. She is too young to work in Germany.

The Sabres left Lynn with a trailer carrying £1,800's worth of equipment for Harwich. From there they go by boat to the Hook of Holland and then to Hamburg.

In the last few weeks, the group have added a twelve-string guitar to their line up — the first in this area to do so.

They have been in existence for two years beginning as "Tony and the Starlights", but since then there have been several changes in personnel.

"We never expected this when we began, but we are very, very pleased with it and proud to be the first from this area to do this," said Tony.

Members of the group are Tony Relph (lead and rhythm guitar), Maurice Pegg (21), of 42 Wootton Road, Lynn (lead and rhythm guitar); Peter Carter (18), of Yard Farm, Shouldham (bass guitar); Ricky Meek (20), of St. Margaret's Lynn Road, Dersingham; and Denny Raven, alias Barry Leader (22), of 6 Russell Place, Lynn (vocalist).

● BELOW — The Sabres lead up for Germany. Left to right are Peter Carter (bass guitar), Tony Relph (lead guitar and rhythm), Richard Meek (drums, sitting), Denny Raven (vocalist) and Maurice Pegg (lead guitar and rhythm). (GC 2920)

The Sabres a hit in Germany

The popular Sabres, second in our contest and whose name was mentioned more than any other group on entry forms, are pictured here outside the "Top Ten" Club in Hamburg — reading the "Lynn News and Advertiser". They are appearing at the club for a month.

The boys — Tony Relph (Shouldham), "Mo" Pegg (Lynn), Peter Carter (Shouldham), Ricky Meek (Dersingham) and Denny Raven (Lynn) — are playing in the club that started The Beatles off.

And you know what that led to!

A missive from the lads tells us that a great time is being had by all. And the Sabre Sound has been a hit with the Germans.

"We have been asked to stay another month, but have decided to return to England, as the work seems to be piling up," they tell us. "We expect to return in the summer and will be cutting a record for the German market then."

The Sabres went out at the beginning of this month. Well done lads!

Press Cuttings circa 1964

THE YOUNG SET
The Sabres are back from Top Ten Club

WONDERFUL TIME IN HAMBURG

JUST back from Hamburg, Germany, after a four-week "smash hit" engagement at the fabulous Top Ten Club are the local group — The Sabres.

With TV appearances, an L.P. recording session and a return booking in Hamburg ahead of them, these five young men have their sights set on a successful career in show business.

The Sabres: Tony Relph (lead and rhythm guitar), "Mo" Pegg (lead and rhythm guitar), Ricky Meek (drums), Peter Carter (bass guitar) and Denny Raven (vocalist) left England in early February.

They travelled by car via Harwich and the Hook of Holland and through the Netherlands into Germany.

TRAILER

Trailing behind their car was a trailer loaded with £1,800 worth of equipment. The journey was not as smooth as they anticipated for while driving through Germany they looked behind their car to see the trailer with its precious cargo dragging along on its side.

This was just one mishap they encountered — it cost them a new tyre, inner... they could even begin to entertain the German fans.

THE SABRES — after a successful four-week engagement at the Top Ten Club in... Raven (vocalist), and "Mo" Pegg (right) are Tony Relph (lead and rhythm guitar, Denny guitar) are... (lead and rhythm). Front row are Peter Carter (bass ...d Ricky Meek (drums). (GC 3321).

33

The Sabres - August 1964
with Issy Bond
L to R Al Drake, Tony Relph, Issy Bond, Tony Pull, Rick Meek, Denny Raven and Pete Carter

Recording The Sabres EP at Bayes Recording Studio October 1964

Hamburg's Reeperbahn - 1964 with 'Top Ten Club' in background

Cartoon Caricatures by Bill Booth - 1964

Rick Circa 1964

On the quayside -
Al Drake, Tony Pull
& Pete Carter - 1964

'Danger'
Loading The Van!

The Sabres
trailer on the
quayside

The Surfin' Sabres 1966
L to R Tony Carter, Richard Sexton, Rick Meek, Tony Relph and Derrick Brunton

The Original 'Three Piece Sweet' 1967
L to R Pete Carter, Rick Meek & Al Drake

with Lionel Francis far right 1968

Chapter Seven – Riding On A High (March 1964 – November 1964)

I flew into Heathrow on Monday March 2nd and made my way back to Norfolk, feeling elated, flush with our success and confident that the big breakthrough the band desperately needed was only just round the corner.
The Sabres had made a lot of friends and contacts in Germany. Decca Records were talking to Peter Eckhorn of the possibility of a live recording series from the club, with albums and singles being released throughout Europe. Peter was already in the process of building a studio at the rear of the club, and had said before we left, he wanted to feature us on the first release, and all of this should be up and running by the time we returned on July 1st. We also had offers of work in Berlin and Frankfurt, plus other interesting opportunities that were worth pursuing. I suppose looking back that although we all wanted to have a hit record and be famous; we were not prepared to deal with the complexities of the music industry and really needed a trusting management to look after everything, and a booking agent to sell the band particularly with the likelihood of more work abroad.
Tony and the rest of the band also arrived back in England on that same day after an uneventful journey home, but this all changed just outside Ipswich as they negotiated a hump-back bridge, on glancing back Tony saw they no longer had a trailer, turning round quickly, the trailer was spotted still lumbering along in the middle of the road with other road users narrowly missing it!
I had managed to save a little bit of money which was good news and my parents were pleased to have me back home, but there was little time to relax, as I had to report back to work the next day. Tony phoned me on my first day back to say the BBC had confirmed our TV appearance for the Friday, which meant asking for a half-day, as we had to be at the studio by 3.00pm, I quickly sorted this minor problem out, and my bosses were surprisingly supportive considering I'd just had almost five weeks off work. We also had a an interview with the local paper, the Lynn News, arranged for Thursday afternoon, but this was not a problem it was Hunstanton early closing day, my normal half day off, thank goodness!
The interview and photograph session went well and we looked forward to our TV spot. We appeared on the evening current events and magazine programme and performed live, with a couple of songs and did a short interview. We got chance to view the film they had shot of us before we left for Hamburg, sadly this has all been lost which is a great shame.
Our first gig on returning home was a local one, at Fincham on March 7th and the place was packed out with our loyal fans. We had a further eight appearances that month stretching from Scottow and Cromer in the east, to King's Lynn and Wisbech in the west.
At the end of March 'Mo' Pegg decided to quit the band mainly for personal reasons, we were sorry to see him go, but the band had to carry on and we soon found a replacement in yet another ex-Escort, Al Drake. Al had been at a loose end since returning from France, he fitted in immediately, and of course it was three quarters of the old Escorts band back together again!
We carried on through April and into May with a succession of great gigs expanding our area of work and evolving our ever changing material, this was a time when blues met soul, and the pop charts were full these songs. We leant songs by many obscure and little known American artists that British bands had success with here, and it

always seemed bizarre to me that this was all happening on the strength of the Beatles amazing worldwide appeal, and the so-called Liverpool sound.

On May 2nd the band made a trip to London to audition for the people who booked the prestigious Flamingo and Whisky-A-Go-Go clubs in London's Wardour Street, this is where Georgie Fame first made his breakthrough. They liked the band and our first appearance was later in May. It was a great gig and we made evermore contacts in our efforts to get the band known.

Because of the many days I was having to take off work, not to mention leaving early to get to some gigs, I had to seriously think about my priorities. My bosses had been more than generous in allowing me to take all this time off, so I decided I had to put the band first and I talked to Reg Brown, handed in my notice, and left on May 16th. We had got quite a bit of work in on the strength of the Hamburg trip and of course we would be heading back once again at the end of June, and I thought it would only be a matter of time before the band would break through nationally.

The other significant event that happened in May was recruiting the talented Offbeats guitarist Tony Pull. Our parents knew each other and I'd known Tony for quite some time; he was also a pretty good keyboard player and could sing as well. We held a band meeting towards the end of May and persuaded Tony Relph to step down as guitarist and act as the band manager, (although he often joined us on the stage) so he could concentrate on getting the band work, manage the money etc, and leave us to just worry about playing the music. With this agreed we set about a reshuffle of the material the band wanted to play, certainly more soul and blues based, and dropping some of the older rock n' roll. We also mapped out the direction we wanted the band to be heading, firstly we felt we had to add keyboards, so I talked to Tony Pull and put these ideas to him, he was interested straight away and decided to take up our offer and join the band. This was great news and with this line-up felt confident that we would have a great band to take back to the Top Ten.

The next thing we had to invest in was better gear, as both Al and Tony played keyboards we bought a Hohner Clavinet keyboard between us, so they could share keyboard duties when needed. Tony already had a Gibson 335 and Selmer amp, and Al had been using an Epiphone Casino for a few months. Pete bought an Epiphone bass and I bought a Slingerland kit in Champagne sparkle that I'd been eyeing up for a while. I nearly got a set of Ludwig's after playing Tea Time Four drummer Rocky Browne's kit, but decided the Slingerland was for me. 'Pully' brought a much needed boast to the band and had a wealth of ideas for new material, he was also in the process of writing some songs which he wanted to try out. He was a perfectionist, keen on blues and jazz, he could play Dave Brubeck's 'Take Five' note for note on piano, but above all he was a great guy with a wicked sense of humour!

The run up to our second visit to Hamburg was as busy as the first, we had to obtain more visas and work permits, and we also suffered the usual delays in having the correct paperwork. On one occasion we all had to go to the German Embassy in London to urgently re-sign some documents, so Jack Barrie lent us his Jaguar. On the return journey, we were all urging Tony Relph to see how fast the Jag would go, with cries of 'come on Relphie, put your foot down', when a roundabout suddenly put itself in front of us and with a grin that only Relphie could do we struck the edge and gently sailed over to land on the top. As we looked down the road there was a local policeman leaning on his bike just scratching his head in disbelieve at the sight he had just witnessed! After checking that no major damage was done to the Jag we continued our journey home and thanked Jack Barrie for the loan of his car!

June was a busy month with ten bookings to fulfil before leaving for the Top Ten around the 28th. We were looking forward to working with the Merseybeats and were booked to share the bill with them in Gt Yarmouth. We had been in London and were a little late in leaving and trying to make up time, but on the Norwich ring road, while trying to corner too fast, the trailer pulled us right over to the other side of the road and we hit the grass bank with a thud. We all hopped out to see if any damage was done, luckily the trailer had remained upright and still attached to the car, but as we were about to hop back into the car again, a police patrol car rolled up, they had seen what had happened and decided Tony was driving without due care and attention. Despite pleading our innocence, Tony was booked and by the time all details were taken, we really were late in getting to Yarmouth. The Mersybeats had to go on first and were not pleased to have the Sabres 'topping the bill'. News was coming in from Iain Hines that the recording studio was nearing completion and we should be able to record some tracks for the first album, something we were really looking forward to. Iain also confirmed that the Blues System would be sharing the bill with us, plus singer Jackie Lynton, who recently had a couple of chart entries, including a top twenty hit with bizarrely *Teddy Bears Picnic*. The top German band the Rackets would also be doing a week or so. All in all it looked like a busy trip!

After playing Lincoln on June 27th we headed back to Germany, this time the weather was hot and sunny and we were determined to work hard and keep pushing the band forward. Issy Bond greeted us with the news that 'Jackie Lynton was a gas' having worked with him before. Jack as we got to call him certainly did live up to Issy's description; he was a charismatic performer a sort of Joe Cocker on speed! He had a great voice and did these jumpy hand movements that had to be seen to be believed!

Issy and Jackie would be singing separate sets with the band, plus Iain and Rikki Barnes would also be adding their talents. We got down to rehearsals and soon put some numbers together. Jack bunked down with us in the top dorm, he was a lazy sod who rarely got out of bed until it was time to go on stage, but once on stage he was magic and much underrated, and after a successful solo career he fronted blues band Savoy Brown for a while.

There were always a lot of characters in Hamburg, we got very friendly with Gigi a very successful 60's model who was often photographed in the pages of the 'Daily Mirror', then there was Ronata, who it was alleged was once, one of Paul McCartney's girlfriends, she told us some amazing stories (most unprintable) about the Beatles early years in Hamburg. The 'Daily Mirror' music critic came over to interview the bands at the Top Ten and got more than he bargained for when we got him drunk, and he was last seen in the arms of two buxom blondes 'whispering he was in love and wanted to marry both of them'

Cliff Bennett & The Rebel Rousers were at the Star Club and we got to hang out with them, Ritchie Blackmore was also in Hamburg, rumoured to be putting a new band together and would pop into the club from time to time.

I got friendly with a German girl named Ursula, who had a flat in an upmarket Hamburg suburb. She would cook me these exotic German dishes, (well exotic to me) which certainly made a change from the 'Mambo' bratwursts. Ursula had a great collection of jazz records, and we'd listen to Dave Brubeck, Miles Davis and Sonny Rollins. I met her father who told me that during the war he was manning the heavy guns that were trying to protect the Port of Hamburg, it seemed a bit surreal to be chatting calmly about these horrific events that affected the many ordinary lives of the German people.

One morning after our last set the band headed off to the Baltic Coast for Travemunde, which had a beautiful golden beach. It was close to the East German border, and Penemunde which was the launch site of the V2 rockets, so close in fact you could see the watchtowers. (In those days Germany of course was divided into the West and the Communist East and had a high security fence, with watchtowers the length of the country). After a day getting rather sunburnt, we only just made it back in time for our first set. We had a visitor from Norfolk, Riv Whisker, the brother of my childhood friend Norman. He was in the Merchant Navy, and with his ship in port he called in at the Top Ten to look me up, he invited us to visit his ship, so the next day we all went down to the port for some great navy hospitality!

On another occasion after the club closed, Iain Hines took a bunch of us out drinking and we all got really drunk on schnapps and we somehow ended up in the early morning market, the only thing I can recall is someone buying a massive bunch of bananas and trying to push them one by one into Al Drakes mouth!

The recording studio had been built in a former dressing room next to the bar and was almost completed when we arrived back at the end of June; there were just some pre-amps and re-verb units to be set up by a guy named Pepe Rush, a Londoner of wide girth who adored his mother. Pepe's claim to fame was that he had developed an echo unit, which he had sold to the British amp manufacture WEM and called the 'Wem Rush Pep Box'.

With this work completed we did some test recordings with Issy and a French singer named Claude Duval. We then recorded two or three other numbers that Peter Eckhorn had suggested. These recording sessions were usually done straight after the club closed, the idea was to issue a series of 'live' recordings which Decca were to put out, but because of the licensing laws which forbid live recordings from the club, the live audience sound was dubbed on later by ourselves, the bar staff and anyone else we could get hold of. Some of these tracks were issued on Live From The Top Ten Beat Club Vol 1 (Decca SLK 16330-P), including *Something Else,* and a couple of tracks of the band backing singer Claude Duval. We also did some publicity photo shoots of the band on stage, and one of these shots was subsequently used for a short time on a series of singles which were released, we were only paid a session fee for all the recordings we made and never received any royalties from sales.

We were filmed at the club by a German TV station, who were putting together a programme on English bands working in Hamburg. We were also approached by a Berlin club owner about the possibility of working there in early '65, and a guy who reportedly owned a club in Rio de Janeiro offered us a two month contract, the pay wasn't bad, but he wouldn't help out with our air fares or accommodation, so we dropped out of that one. Issy had got pretty tight with us and worked with the band more and more, she had some time off planned, so decided to come over to England in mid August and spend a couple of weeks with us, to take in the sights and do a few gigs with the band. We played into the first few days of August and returned home after another triumphant visit to Hamburg. We would be heading back again at the end of October, with a further month pencilled in for the following April. The band had fifteen bookings for the month of August, and Issy would be joining us around the 15th. Word soon got out about her visit and we did a photo/interview session for a couple of local newspapers. Anglia TV picked this up and phoned Tony Relph to see if we would be able to appear on their magazine programme 'About Anglia', going out live on August 21st; we didn't take long to answer yes! Anglia wanted us to perform two or three songs and also to feature Issy Bond. The band did a couple of songs and Issy sang *Baby, Baby* (*Where Did Our Love Go*)' which she had recorded and released as a single in Germany. We had a great time doing this and the Presenters, Bob Wellings and Chris Kelly (who later went on to become a well known TV games host) took us out for a drink afterwards.

This TV appearance gave the band a terrific boast and we would spend our breaks signing autographs wherever we went. Issy went back to Germany at the end of August, and we continued working round the country in September and October ready to return for our third visit to the Top Ten.

We had a few prestige dates to look forward to; among them was a shared bill at Cromer with Lulu & The Luvers. Lulu was riding high with her hit *Shout* and came from Glasgow, and knew Issy quite well. She was great, but back then I little realised what a massive international star she would become. We chatted and had photographs taken, which I think Mary Relph still has. Another show we did at Peterborough was with the Honeycombs, who had a huge hit with *Have I The Right*. Honey Langtree was the drummer in the group, (which was very unusual in 1964) not much of a drum technician I had to sort out her bass drum pedal and lend her my drum stool, however the gig was memorable because a crowd of guys who were taunting Honey managed to pull their guitarist off the stage, and I believe breaking his leg in the process!

We had our regular nights at the Maids Head, and as the title of this book implies the Maids Head will always be associated with the local band scene of the 60's, it was perhaps King's Lynn's answer to Liverpool's Cavern Club. The landlord Colin Atkinson was always an enthusiastic supporter of the band and we probably played there more than any other venue. Colin or 'Acky' as he was affectionately known played a big part in launching the musical careers of Tea Time Four's, Boz Burrell and Barry 'Fats' Dean. Boz of course went on to join Robert Fripp's King Crimson, before moving on to form Bad Company with Paul Rodgers, as they say the rest is history. Barry Dean spent some time with the Brian Auger Oblivion Express, recording several albums with Auger in the 70's. They were a groundbreaking vocal/ fusion band that gave Herbie Hancock's Headhunters a run for their money. 'Fats' proved to be an innovative composer, as well as an outstanding bassist.

Another Norfolk musician who did rather well was Watton's Mike Patto, Mike use to frequent venues that we played, and often used to get up with us and sing a couple of songs, but he would have to wait until the 70's before he gained considerable success on forming the band Patto with guitarist Ollie Halsall, releasing a string of great albums, sadly Mike died when he was only in his early thirties.

Before leaving for Hamburg we got down to recording some tracks at Bob Booth's recording studio. The studio was situated above Bob's record shop in Tower Street, King's Lynn. (there really should be a blue plaque to honour this) Bob was, and still is an enthusiastic music lover with an encyclopaedic memory for all details of just about anything to do with pop music. Bob always wanted to build a recording studio, record and release the records himself. He knew what sounded good and possessed the natural talent required to achieve this, by the time of recording Denny Raven (Barry) was no longer in the band, we had parted amicably with him and he came to the studio to lend a hand (he later went on to join another band and return to Hamburg, before dropping out of music altogether). We finally recorded four tracks on October 16th, *Can I Get A Witness, Rock n'roll Music, I'll Try* and a song written by the band *No Time For You* These four tracks were released as <u>The Sabres EP</u> at the end of November 1964. After playing the Gala at Norwich on October 27th we got ready to pack for Hamburg. No more losing the trailer on route, Tony was taking no chances, we had a van this time and the band were really going places and it seemed nothing could go wrong! Could it?

Chapter Eight – Rock Bottom (November 1964 – March 1965)

Once again we were back on the Reeperbahn and looking forward to five weeks at the Top Ten. Right at the start I knew this would be a month to remember, we had built up a sizeable following in the year, and it seemed on the first night all our friends and fans were there to welcome us back and queues were forming outside waiting for the doors to open.

For the most part we would be sharing the stage with the Alex Harvey Soul Band from Glasgow, Alex Harvey was much loved in Hamburg and his drinking capacity became legendary, by 1964 he had already been in bands for ten years and was a seasoned pro with a great soul voice. It would take him a further ten years to gain international stardom as the Sensational Alex Harvey Band; he formed with Zal Cleminson's band Teargas. Among their hits was a manic version of Tom Jones's *Delilah* that could only be described as 'early punk'. His younger brother Les was also in his band, Les later formed Stone The Crows with Maggie Bell, he later died tragically after being electrocuted on stage in Swansea before a concert with the 'Crows' in 1972.

Alex and Les were part of the Glasgow clan of musicians that included Bill and Bobby Patrick, Lulu, Rikki Barnes, Issy Bond and Maggie Bell among others. Also appearing for a couple of weeks was a New York based all girl group Goldie & The Gingerbreads, who ex-Animal Chas Chandler had brought over to Europe to promote. Chandler was often in the Top Ten and showed interest in the Sabres, but unfortunately nothing came of this, who knows what might have happened, or was I just dreaming! The Gingerbreads were unique, in the fact they were the first (as far as I know) all girl rock group who could sing and play their own instruments, they were pretty good too! After releasing a couple of singles like so many 60's bands they faded into oblivion.

Peter Eckhorn had fine tuned his recording studio and wanted to record the Sabres with special guests and release a single, and also to include some tracks perhaps for future release in the 'Top Ten Live' series of albums. Iain Hines suggested pulling John Lee Hooker's *Hoochie Coochie Man* apart and putting a new slant to it. Tony Pull would do lead vocals and we got together a few times to pool ideas. In the end we came up with a mix of *Hit The Road Jack* and *Hi Heel Sneakers* type rhythms. Iain added Hammond B3 with Rikki Barnes on Tenor Sax, and Alex Harvey and Issy Bond came in and helped out on backing vocals. We spent a long time getting everything just right and recorded several versions before the final take. We were all pleased with the end result, it sounded pretty good and was different enough to catch on. We sorted through some other songs and a couple that Tony Pull was in the early stages of writing, but in the end all of this was held on a back burner, with the idea of putting these down on our next visit to the Top Ten the following April.

It was not all work though, the fair was in town with dodgems and all the usual rides, and Ursula took me down there on a couple of afternoons to unwind. Christmas was only just round the corner and the centre of Hamburg was festooned with decorations and Christmas trees with pretty lights, all the shops had massive displays of gifts and everywhere you went, seemed like one big party!

This party atmosphere never left the Top Ten even when it wasn't the run up to Christmas, but our November visit seemed special. The time whirled by so quickly, as each day blurred into another. Tony Sheridan spent most evenings in the club, when he wasn't working, he was a big friend of Alex Harvey and usually got up with his band to sing a few numbers, this progressed into an all-star jam in the last couple of weeks, with Harvey and Sheridan joining the Sabres on stage, together with Iain and Rikki, and sometimes Issy as well. This was a fantastic band and I only wish we had recorded some of these sessions. We tried to get Chas Chandler on stage, but he always refused saying he was now into management, and of course it wasn't too long before he discovered Jimi Hendrix and made him a worldwide super-star.

We left the Top Ten for home on December 4th with a firm contract to return the following April, but little realised as we left in a snow storm that this would be our final visit. We stayed overnight in Holland and got back to King's Lynn the next evening. At first it was good to be back home in time for the Christmas celebrations with time to relax with friends and family.

I looked through the diary and quickly realised a distinct lack of bookings, we had failed to break into the London scene and our travels outside of East Anglia were few and far between. It was true that we were very popular in Hamburg and with the hopeful release of a single and other tracks to be included on the first Top Ten album, all planned for early 1965 release, there was much to look forward to, but what were we going to live on until next April?

We had hoped that we could have found work in other clubs in Berlin, Frankfurt or Hanover, but none of the initial enquiries had led to anything. Other clubs were not as good as Peter Eckhorn's Top Ten, either the money wasn't enough or we would have to pay accommodation, the other offers from South America seemed dodgy on reflection and it was a long way to come home if anything went wrong.

Our first gig on arriving home was at March on December 7th, with a further six to complete the month's work. There was some good news however, Bob Booth had released the EP of our October recordings and sales were encouraging. It was on the Whisky juke box and being played constantly, Bob had also managed to get it onto several local pub juke boxes as well, and this all helped generate sales to keep the Sabres name out front!

Tony Relph worked flat out in trying to get gigs in for early 1965, but despite the success of the Sabres in Hamburg it was still proving to be a difficult task. Partly because we had been out of the Country for at least four months in 1964, but also because we had cancelled quite a lot of work scheduled ahead to fit round our Hamburg visits, and a lot of promoters, agents etc naturally felt let down and were reluctant to re-book the band in case we cancelled them out again. I think even regular gigs for people we could call our friends, all thought we had just dropped them in our search to reach the top and now that we were desperate for work, thought why should we bother now! All of these problems seemed to creep up on us and we were ill prepared to deal with them. Looking back, I can now clearly see why we got ourselves into these difficulties. We were no different to the many successful bands that achieved a degree of fame in Hamburg, but failed to break though in their homeland.

January looked a make or break month with only three gigs to start off with. Tony managed to get two more gigs at the NCO Club, Lakenheath. But after that there was nothing firmly booked until we returned to Hamburg in April. Tony tried all the agents he knew, to see if we could fill a couple of months working the American bases in Europe, but there was nothing imminent, or available. This was disastrous news and with no money coming in, how long could the band last. We played the couple of gigs at Lakenheath in the final week of January and then held a band meeting to see if we could salvage anything. The band had never played better and after all the hard work we had put into it, we couldn't just give up, but we were getting despondent and it seemed like a big hole had opened up and was swallowing us all up. Tony said he would give it one more try to get the band some work and we decided to meet up again the first week in February, to decide what we should do, there just wasn't a quick fix solution. When we met up, Tony had only managed to get one more gig, and that wasn't until the middle of March. How could all of this be happening when it seemed just six months ago everybody wanted to book the Sabres. We had reached rock bottom and reluctantly felt we could no longer carry on, all the drive and enthusiasm had been knocked out of us. We cancelled the one remaining gig and then phoned Iain Hines in Hamburg to tell him the bad news that the band had broken up and would not be returning to the Top Ten in April. Iain and Peter tried to persuade us to carry on, but the decision had been taken.

To put it mildly, I was completely devastated and it seemed that all of my dreams had been pulled from underneath me. Tony Relph had always done his best, it wasn't any fault on his part, but I felt completely let down, we all did and for a while it was difficult to cope with. I didn't go far in those first weeks after the band split and didn't contact the rest of the band. My mum was worried what I was going to do, and my dad was urging me to get a job – any job and quickly, but pride got in my way and to be honest, it was the last thing I wanted to do. I struggled on with no money coming in and the little I had saved from the Top Ten rapidly depleting. Towards the end of February I realised I had only two choices, either go to London, rough it and try to get into a band, or stay in Norfolk, get a job to get me by and look for a local band that needed a drummer and start all over again. In the end I knew that going to London or anywhere else for that matter was not an option. I hadn't made any payments on my drum kit for months and it was about to be reclaimed back by the loan company. My car was now off the road because I couldn't afford to tax and insure it, and I was also two or three months behind in car loan payments. So reluctantly I choose to stay put and sort out my mess, firstly I phoned Reg Brown to see if there was any work he could put my way. He had just lost two members of staff and he offered me a few weeks work until he found replacements, and I could start immediately. I was grateful, at least I could get a little money rolling in.

In early March my drums were repossessed, despite my pleas for more time to pay. I asked my dad if he would lend me the money, but he was adamant and refused saying I had got myself into this mess and I had to get out of it myself. I understood his reasons, I couldn't keep expecting others to bail me out every time I got into difficulties, but I still felt depressed and angry and thought I had lost everything and all I ever wanted was to be a successful musician.

At the end of March I had an unexpected call from Paul Chris, to see if I would be interested in joining an offshoot of his own band, to be called the Mark Anthony Band. As he had such a lot of work coming in for the Paul Chris Band, he decided to form an alternative unit for the extra gigs and work two bands. I explained the fact I had no drums, he said he'd help. Paul gave me some cymbals and I managed to find an old second-hand Premier kit at Nigel Portass's newly opened music shop, and I was back in business again. I was not too sure how this new band would work out or what type of music I would be playing, but I will always remember Paul for his generosity and kindness at a low point in my life and for giving me the encouragement to hang in and not to give up.

Chapter Nine – Finding My Way Back (April 1965 – October 1970)

The Mark Anthony Band was an oddball and lasted less than a year. Both Al Drake and Tony Pull, (before he opted for a spell on the assembly line at Vauxhall Motors in Luton) were part of the line up at sometime during the year. Tony later moved to London and spent some time playing guitar for 60's singing star Clodagh Rodgers, who had notched up a couple of number one hits. Other band members included sax player Garth Coles a wonderful character, who I got to know well and was to play many gigs with during the years ahead. George Ragsdale was on trumpet, with Brian Coggles on bass, occasionally singer Valerie Bond would be added to the line up.

This was a completely different band than I'd been used to, more Showband style with strict tempo rhythms which was a novelty at first, but enjoyable nonetheless and it gave a chance to get my jazz chops together. The band played numbers like *Tequila* and *One Mint Julep,* as well as more mundane stuff such as *In The Mood*, but we still managed to inject some rock and soul into the programme.

We first got together for rehearsals in early April and the first gig was at the Officer's Club, Alconbury on April 6th, which really set the pattern for most of our gigs as the Mark Anthony Band. Apart from a couple of odd occasions, all of our work was at RAF and USAF bases, including Marham, Scultborpe, Coltishall, Honnington, Lakenheath, Mildenhall, Bentwaters and Woodbridge. These were gigs passed on by Paul, who was really acting as our booking agent.

I use to look forward to the American clubs, working on these airbases was like a mini America, you had to change your money because everything was sold in $US. We were allowed to eat and drink in the clubs, but nothing could be bought and taken away. I had of course played these clubs a few times with the Sabres, but it was these visits that gave me my first taste of hamburgers, Jack Daniels and Bud beer. Also the vast breakfasts that were served after the clubs closed on a Friday and Saturday nights were legendary, with such delights as corn beef hash and pancakes with maple syrup. I made up my mind to visit America as soon as possible, it seemed a magical land offering not only the best music and untold culinary delights, but also a wealth of endless new pleasures and my love of America is still ongoing today and as strong as ever.

We didn't play that many gigs during the year, so when Tony Relph phoned in December to say he was thinking of reforming the Sabres, as the Surfin' Sabres, I jumped at the chance to re-join him. Surfing music was now riding high in the charts with the Beach Boys seemingly overtaking the Beatles in the popularity stakes. In the year since the Sabres had split, Tony had taught himself to play the sax and he proved to be a reasonable tenor sax player. The line up was Tony (sax & vocals), Richard Sexton (guitar & vocals), Derrick Brunton (guitar & vocals) and Tony Cater (bass & vocals).

The new version of the Sabres was as different from the original as could be with the emphasis firmly on the vocal harmonies. We rehearsed through January 1966 with the first gig at Brandon on January 30th.

The surfin' sounds proved popular even though the band was short lived. We worked around East Anglia from Great Yarmouth and Norwich and as far as the Ipswich and Colchester areas. Of course some of the work was more localised in King's Lynn, Swaffham and Downham Market. We played mostly Beach Boys material, but as the year progressed we added popular soul type songs, such as *Barefootin'* and *Get Out'a My Life Woman*.

In March I married Maggie Eagle, we had first met during the height of the Sabres popularity in the summer of 1964, when Maggie's older sister Carol, was Tony Pull's girlfriend.

Tony Relph's ambition was to open a club and model it on Hamburg's Top Ten. He found a suitable place in of all places Feltwell, near Thetford, not the most ideal location perhaps, (although it did have the US bases close by) but nonetheless it worked for a time. The building was an old cinema, complete with a stage. Tony named it 'The Crazy Horse Club' and started up a Sunday club, with the Surfin' Sabres as the resident band, and a guest band would be booked most weeks as well. Barry Lee & The Planets from North Walsham were popular (this was long before they achieved national fame as the Brother Lee's) and they played the club almost as many times as we did. In the end it proved too costly to keep running and Tony was forced to close it down before the end of the year, but he had at least achieved his dream and it was a popular music venue for a few months in 1966.

I met up with Boz Burrell on Liverpool St Station one August afternoon; we were both waiting for the King's Lynn train. We shared the journey over a few beers and he talked about his solo career, which he wasn't too keen on. I think he might have even quit if he hadn't eventually joined King Crimson. We had a laugh and it was good to see him and we kept in contact intermittingly through the years ahead.

The highlight of the year was a big event held at the Grafton Club, RAF Marham with three or four bands. Status Quo was the headlining band and the place was packed full. Another memorable gig was at Heacham Public Hall, where we shared the bill with Family who were very much in their infancy back then, but I remember they were a fabulous band with Roger Chapman (vocals), Ric Grech (bass), Charlie Whitney (guitar), Jim King (sax) and of course Rob Townsend (drums). Tony Ashton (keyboards) might have also been there, I seem to recall some electric piano. Apart from their original songs, they did a wonderful version of Junior Walker's *I'm A Roadrunner*, great friendly guys too. We also played a few society gigs, including a coming-out ball for Lord Fisher at Kilverstone and a big event at Felbrigg Hall, near Cromer.

The Surfin' Sabres split up at the end of the year, no particular reason; it had just run its course. In early 1967 Al Drake and I got together to see if we could form a guitar based trio, we would of course play rock and chart songs, but work was slowly changing and to survive you had to be versatile and add a degree of dance / showband type material. We didn't want to sound old fashioned, but thought with careful choice of songs we could pull this off and get the gigs that fell into that middle territory, that was both eclectic and popular at the same time.

During the two years since the original Sabres split, Pete Carter had spent sometime in Germany working with a band at various clubs. While there he had met and married a German girl. After the band returned home, Pete stayed on in Germany and to get some money together had got a job on a German fishing boat that fished the arctic water around Iceland, before he returned to England in early 1967.

Al and I put the idea of a new band to Pete and he agreed to join us, we thought up numerous names to call ourselves and eventually came up with the name Three Piece Sweet, it kinda' rolled off the tongue and sounded quirky, just like us!

We bought a PA system between us, and discussed songs we wanted to put in the set list. We didn't need much rehearsal time, we had dozens of numbers in the songbook and Al had this encyclopaedic musical brain, which seemed to have every song that had ever been written, firmly entrenched in his mind with words and key always to hand, it was really uncanny.

During 1967 we slowly got the band known and we were right in being versatile, bookings went from one a week to an average of three or four, sometimes five. Depending on the age and type of gig we could easily switch the programme around. We got a residency at the Palm Court Bar, which at that time was part of the Globe Hotel, King's Lynn. During the late 60's the American base at Sculthorpe was still operating and had several hundred personnel, they would come into town and chat up the local girls, whose boyfriends were to say a little jealous, and at times full scale fights would develop with bottles, chairs and tables flying in all directions. We still worked regularly at RAF and USAF bases and clubs like the Tyneside at Sherringham and the many Peterborough clubs.

By 1968 we were being asked for a larger band, so we recruited Lionel 'Frisky' Francis, a trumpet player who had been in the Paul Chris Band. He would join us on some of our gigs. This presented a problem with the band name, so for any gigs with Lionel we would call ourselves the Ricky Allen Band, (easily combining Al's and my name together) with this larger line up we were able to get more private functions and other prestigious gigs. I took most of the bookings and got to know a lot of people, I was still friendly with Paul Chris, who recommended the band for numerous gigs. 1968 was the year I got to know Tom Legge and Geoff Searle from Searles Holiday Park at Hunstanton, as well as booking the band there I also did some freelance work at the club with other local musicians, including Dorothy MacDonald, the loudest pianist I have ever worked with. She was a very popular figure at Searles and always went down well with the holidaymakers.

In August my son Nick was born, it was to be a busy summer with a new member of the family to bring up and find the time to be with him. Life was busy, I had been through numerous jobs since early 1965, but in 1968 I had found a job I enjoyed as a used car salesman at W H King, King's Lynn. I had got the job through Al Drake and Paul Chris who both worked there as salesmen.

King's provided a car with plenty of free petrol, which we used as band transport. I usually had a Ford Cortina and with the back seat removed and huge boot we could get all the band gear loaded in, with the three of us in the front with a cushion between the seats (no seat belts in those days). King's also provided many humorous moments like the time I brought a car back from being totally re-sprayed, only to scrape all the side after turning too sharply into the garage forecourt and colliding with the wall, or falling asleep in the back of the car on a warm summer's day and being woken by the manager, who was non too happy at the time, but life at King's was generally happy even if I didn't earn that much money and had to work six days a week!

We did a lot of work for the new companies that were relocating to King's Lynn in the late 60's including Campbell's Soups, Tennon Contracts, Dornay Foods and John Bamber Engineering. They all set up social clubs and Tennon's even built their own clubhouse on the Hardwick Estate. We became almost the house band at Tennon's and would back cabaret shows and especially the stag nights, which were as you can imagine extremely popular. I think Tennon was the first to present high-class London strippers in the King's Lynn area and of course the band looked forward to these intellectual evenings!

By 1969 we were doing more and more private functions, so to create a fuller sound, we also added Geoff Hopkinson on keyboards for a lot of our gigs. We were still working the trio, but went out as a quintet more often as our popularity increased.

These were the days of ballroom dancing and we used to do a regular spot at the Majestic in King's Lynn, which before it was made into the multi-screen cinema of today, had a magnificent ballroom with regular Saturday dances. These were not my favourite gigs as all the strict tempo stuff could be very limiting and extremely boring, and we were always being asked for some obscure dance we'd never heard of like the 'Northumberland square tango' or something like that!

I also recall doing a large event for Campbell's Soups at the Kit Kat, Hunstanton, this was in the days of spot waltzes and we proceeded to give away a pile of prizes that were lying alongside the stage, only to be told that they were all raffle prizes for the yearly draw. Campbell's were not too happy as we had given away expensive watches, gift vouches and even a camera, but how were we to know!

In 1969 I bought my first house on the outskirts of King's Lynn, the band work and car sales were both picking up and with Nick now walking we really needed a garden for him to run around in. We also had a dog; a golden Labrador named 'Henry' who would play a big part in our lives.

So as the 60's gave way to the 70's life carried on much the same with the band still working an average of fifteen or more gigs a month and just as popular as ever.

In February Steve Tegg the bassist in the Paul Chris Band made an unexpected visit to see me at work. He told me Paul wanted to see me urgently and was in his car outside. I wondered why he had not called in himself. I hadn't seen much of him since he had left King's to concentrate on his band in the summer of the previous year and had taken the band to Spain, touring the American bases.

I was shocked when I saw Paul, he looked ill and tired, he quickly told me he had to check into hospital urgently that morning for suspected cancer. He had almost collapsed the previous evening while the band was playing at Hunstanton. Paul was taken to hospital then, but he had insisted on discharging himself to sort out how the band was going to carry on without a drummer. He showed me the band diary and asked me to fill in for him on as many dates as possible, which I readily agreed. There were several mid-week dates where I was free, plus an odd weekend date. I dropped everything to play that night at Bentwaters NCO club. Paul had a huge reputation as a bandleader and had attracted some top London musicians to the band. The line-up was three horns, keyboards, guitar, bass, drums and a girl singer who as a 'Penthouse Pet' had recently displayed all as a centre spread 'Pet' of the month.

This band was great to work with and I quickly had to learn all the horn accents as well as new material I had never played before, such as Blood, Sweat & Tears *Spinning Wheel* with its complicated stop starts and tempo changes, but it was enormous fun and a challenge I locked into. I worked fourteen consecutive nights, including the gigs with Ricky Allen, most of which were long distance, late nights. I did a further two or three gigs with the band when the sad news of Paul's death came through. I was shocked and stunned; it just didn't seem possible that at just 40 years old Paul could be dead. His family and close band members all thought he had been hiding his illness and choose to ignore it until finally this was not possible. Over the years Paul had been a good friend, he was generous man who would always go out of his way to help anyone and when he needed helping, it was not to be.

Paul's funeral was held at St.John's church, King's Lynn and I went with Johnny Byles the Norwich sax player, who had been in Paul's band and Anglia TV's Peter Fenn. The church was packed with friends and fellow musicians and Paul's obituary was even reported in the 'Melody Maker'.

The band was to carry on with Steve Tegg taking over as leader; they had a lot of work and were due to return to Spain in the summer. Steve and the rest of the band wanted me to join, but I felt I couldn't, I had a diary full of bookings with our own band and was still working my day job.

We held a memorial evening at the Dukes Head, King's Lynn to raise money for Paul's widow Mavis and young son. Paul's band, together with Ricky Allen gave our services free and we were able to raise a considerable sum to help the family.

In May I decided to leave W H King. Dudley Keys the manager who I had always liked and got on with had left, and a new manager appointed. We had a clash of personalities; it was time to leave, so I picked up a second-hand Cortina at trade price and concentrated on being a full time musician once more. With the band work and various other freelance jobs with other bands, I felt secure, at least in the short term of being able to put food on the table. Occasionally I would lend a hand in my parent's newspaper shop in St James Street, King's Lynn, which they had taken over in late 1967.

In July I decided to trade in my Cortina for a new Fiat van, which would be large enough for all the band gear without being cramped. The van had a separate cab and was flat fronted and I momentarily thought not much protection in an accident, how those thoughts would echo true!

The summer rolled by quickly and the band was as busy as ever. I bought Joe Cocker's 'Mad Dogs & Englishmen' and we played several songs from the album that became very popular on the US bases where the band constantly worked.

On October 15th we were working at the NCO club at Mildenhall, just a regular Thursday night gig. I packed up and left with Pete Carter shortly before midnight. I was driving on the Brandon road alongside Lakenheath airbase when a car suddenly shot into view from nowhere, being driven very fast, all I could see were these bright headlights coming towards me and all too late I realised….on the wrong side of the road! I tried desperately to avoid a collision, but it was too late. The car slammed straight into me, head-on and slightly to the right, I took the full force of the impact. There was a horrendous crash and sound of tearing metal. Time seemed to stop still and then everything was happening in slow motion, the front windscreen seemed to just slowly drop away and then deadly silence. I remained conscious throughout and quickly realised I was in tremendous pain and couldn't move, the cab had crumpled around me and I was trapped. Pete was lucky and had managed to avoid the worst of the impact and could move. I put my hand down and could feel something warm and sticky and realised it was blood – my blood. It was only then that I could feel myself lapsing in and out of unconsciousness. Someone was at the side and was trying to force open my door to get me out, but couldn't, he put his arm through the broken windscreen and held my hand telling me I would be okay, help was coming. I later found out he was a taxi driver and I will always remember his kindness. He was able to radio through to his base to alert the emergency services and there is no doubt his quick response helped save my life. The front of the Fiat was completely caved in on my side and I was trapped between this and the panel that separated the cab from the loading section, at least this kept all the band gear from crashing into me on impact, the only thing I could move was my right hand and wrist.

The ambulance, police and fire service were all on the scene quickly, but it took well over an hour to release me, and of course there was always the risk of fire.

I was rushed to Newmarket General Hospital for emergency surgery; I had potential life threatening injuries and had lost a great deal of blood, in my semi-conscious haze I realised that both my legs were completely shattered!

Chapter Ten – Picking Up The Pieces (The 1970's)

The police broke the news of my accident to Maggie with a knock on the door at 2.00am, she was five months pregnant with our daughter Rae and this couldn't have come at a worse time. They didn't have much information for her, other than it was serious and I was undergoing emergency surgery at Newmarket General Hospital.
For nearly a week I didn't remember much, at times I realised Maggie, my mum and Maggie's mum were there, but not much else. Initially I had lost a lot of blood, this was obviously quite life threatening and replacing it was the first priority and I had several blood transfusions. My injuries were very serious and complicated and I was in surgery for several hours, in layman's terms I was pretty smashed up. I had severe fractures in both legs, my right thigh had a compound fracture with the bone snapping and coming through the skin, I had a further four breaks in the lower legs, both ankles broken and various other bones in my feet, all toes broken and twisted, plus some damage to my knees and hips.
I clung on to life for the first couple of days, the surgeons were worried about my right leg, which they thought might have to be amputated at one stage, but thanks to their tremendous skills they managed to save it. I was kept sedated on morphine and it wasn't until a week later the gravity of my injuries became apparent to me. For all my family it was an immensely difficult time and being in a hospital forty miles from home did not help the situation. Because of the seriousness of my injuries there was little hope of me being transferred to a hospital nearer home in the foreseeable future? I was in plaster and on traction, unable to move and before Christmas was to have a further three operations.
I suffered panic attacks and realised I may never play drums again, and also wondered if I would ever be able to walk again. I kept getting flashbacks and nightmares of being trapped and unable to move. The love of family and friends somehow kept me going. Maggie came to see me every day with the help of a car rota organised by family and friends, I will always remember their kindness and help at this time and be indebted to Maggie and all the family for the rest of my life for holding everything together at this time. I received what seemed like hundreds of cards and get well messages, a lot from people I didn't even know.
I suffered several setbacks, but was eventually transferred to St James Hospital in King's Lynn shortly before Christmas, and was glad to be nearer home. I had another operation to remove a pin that was in my right knee and to see how my bones were healing. At first everything seemed to be slowly progressing, but after returning to the ward I began suffering severe pains in my right thigh and spent New Years Eve in agony. An x-ray revealed that the bone had pulled away, effectively putting me back to square one again. In the end I had to have my right leg pinned with a metal pin between knee and hip, and plates placed in my ankle to hold everything together. These remain there to today and I have often jokingly said 'if they were ever removed my whole right leg would fall off', my children later dubbed me the original bionic man!
My daughter Rae was born in February, the day before I was finally released from hospital, and I was taken in a wheelchair to see her. It was an emotional moment if things had taken another course I might not have been there to welcome her into the world. In total I had spent nearly twenty weeks in hospital, I would have to return

The Mystery is Solved!
Pete, Rick and Al are super group ESP 1969

'Shame they never wanted us"! - Goldyrocks 1977
L to R Pete Carter, Simon Lilley & Rick Meek

52nd Street playing Jazz at The King's Lynn Arts Festival - 1978
L to R Roy Bentley, Rick Meek, George McKay and Pete Carter

Fooling Around at the Nice Jazz Festival 1978

Yosemite National Park California - 1980

Barrie (right) playing 22 Mandolins!
on stage with Chris Copping

Barrie all dressed up!
for Grand Hotel.

Procol Harum at the time of Grand Hotel

The Good Times!

Nicola & Barrie Wilson with their horses in Oregon - 1980's

L to R Barrie Wilson, Dick Atkinson and me - late 70's

Barrie Wilson relaxing 1980

Me and Barrie - 1980

Sue, Nicola, Sarah & Barrie Wilson
Santa Barbara - 1983

'Still Rockin' early 80's

Disneyland - California
1986

In London - 1982 for Barrie's Gig with Joe Cocker
L to R Barrie Wilson, Kelly Atkinson, Viv Stanshall,
Dick Atkinson & Rick Meek

Maureen and The Three Piece Sweet - early 80's

Last Gig with The Three Piece Sweet
1990

Drinking in the music -
with Colin Bailey *centre*
and Dick Atkinson
early 90's

Some of the Old Gang! meeting
up in 2004
L to R Rick Wilson, Al Drake,
Rick Meek, Tony Relph,
Pete Carter, Dennis Scott
and Mo Drake

Our Travels!

Chrissie & Me in Bali - 1996

Meeting The President late 90's

Volcano watch in Hawaii

61

Original 'Hamburg Days' Story - featured in
Blue Suede News - 2001

Sue Wilson at home in Oregon
2004

Tea at the Savoy-London
catching up when Joe Coleman was in the UK filming "America's Next Top Model"
L to R Joe, Sarah, Rick and Dick - 2005

Maureen & The Three Piece Sweet
early 80's

Rick in Chicago 1993

daily to the hospital to learn how to walk, all over again. The first time I tried was frightening and painful I just didn't know how to, but with the help and encouragement from the nurses over the following weeks I took my first steps. My right leg was nearly an inch and a half shorter than my left and I was left with a pronounced bow to my left leg and a limp, as well as some bent toes and other mobility problems that remain with me to today, but at least I could slowly come to terms with my disabilities and try to move on a day at a time.

The driver of the car that smashed into me was an American Serviceman from Lakenheath. The police told me he might have been drunk, but because he was quickly picked up and taken back to the base, no evidence could be proved. He was eventually prosecuted for careless driving and only fined a few pounds; he had not been seriously injured in the accident. My Fiat was a write off and a couple of drums had been damaged, but the rest of the band gear survived pretty much intact. I only received a minimal insurance payment for the Fiat and injuries. I didn't have the money to sue for my severe injuries and loss of earnings; this was in a day when suing for damages were practically unheard of!

With the help and support of all my family, I slowly made a recovery and by the time of my 28th Birthday on the last day of May, I was walking a few steps with the aid of crutches.

The band had carried on using local drummer John Savage. I didn't know whether I would ever be able to get behind a drum kit again, but the doctors offered encouragement, so it became a goal to achieve. I knew I would never be able to play as before, I had restricted movement and would always have this problem together with leg weakness and pain, but I made a start with gentle exercises. I realised my feet would never ever be able to achieve those intricate bass drum patterns and speed of the past and fatigue would soon set in, but what I lacked in my limbs I could try and make up with my hands, wrists and arms, in effect I reinvented my playing style somewhat!

In late summer I tried to play a few gigs with the Ricky Allen Band, but in the end it just didn't work out. It was too soon for me to be going back playing drums, I needed more recovery time.

In the autumn I bought an old Hillman Estate car and started to drive a little to overcome my fear of getting behind the wheel again. No long distances just short hops. I was a little nervous at first and wasn't sure if my legs were strong enough to be able to drive, but little by little I gained confidence, but the thought of night driving took me a long time to come to terms with and something I've never been able to fully overcome, and even today when I see headlights coming toward me I sometimes get a momentary flashback of that awful accident.

Eventually my thoughts went to trying to form a new band, one that I could organise and pace myself and hopefully slowly ease myself back into playing drums again, and if it didn't work out and I couldn't play again – well I would have to cross that bridge when it came.

I thought nothing heavy or tiring just something to get me started. I knew the Paul Chris Band had recently broken up, unable to keep going after Paul's death. I contacted Steve Tegg to see if he would be interested, not only was he interested he suggested guitarist Ray Potts and singer Jackie Curran, who had both been in Paul's band. I put an advert in the papers for a keyboardist, this brought a response from Peterborough based Trevor Marriott who would join us. So after just over a year I was slowly getting back again, we rehearsed a few times and slowly put a set list together.

I decided to call the band the Rick Keen Sound (in memory of my grandfather Richard Keen Williams). Jackie was a good singer and like Steve, was a Londoner who had moved to King's Lynn to join Paul Chris. We did top forty stuff mixed with a little country, plus some straight ahead standards. Ray as well as being a versatile guitarist was also a good singer and could handle back up vocals for Jackie, Trevor anchored the sound on organ and could also play foot-pedal bass. I contacted friends on the American bases and put some gigs together, although I found it difficult and tiring I was determined to make another go of playing drums and felt I had been given a second chance.

Around this time friends like Mike Williamson and Peterborough drummer Frank Walton took me to Ronnie Scott's club in London, to see one of my drum heroes Buddy Rich. We returned quite a few times over the next two or three years and took in Ella Fitzgerald, Chick Corea, Roland Kirk, and another drum hero of mine, Elvin Jones. I saw Buddy Rich several times at Ronnie's and was there when he recorded a live album from the club, Rich as well as being a an unbelievable drummer was every bit as good as a comedian with a brutally dark sense of humour, talking of which, Cheech & Chong the American comedian/actors appeared at the club on one occasion and brought the house down. I used to meet up occasionally with Mike Patto who was a regular at Ronnie's and we used to people spot famous celebrities who were often in the audience.

I started to be asked to recommend other bands etc for various clubs/functions so I began a small entertainment agency to book other acts out and also gave a few drum lessons, bit by bit I felt I was slowly getting somewhere.

At the end of 1971 Steve moved back to London and was replaced by Mike Donald another ex-Paul Chris musician. The band worked steadily through 1972 with American and RAF bases providing the majority of gigs, but other popular venues such as Eddie Kidd's Country Club at Hunstanton and Ronan Lesley's Anchor Club at Snettisham provided some local work.

On one occasion at the Galaxy Club, Mildenhall we had a request for *Wipeout*, the Surfaris hit. This was not on our set list, but I thought we all knew it, although I had never played it before. I had always thought it was just a steady beat based on single/double stroke rolls on the drum solo section, but when we took a break a guy comes up to me and says 'that's not the way you play drums on *Wipeout*, you've got to use a combination of paradiddle/triplet strokes', (technical here) and proceeded to show me. I said 'who are you? He replied 'I'm Ron Wilson, I played on the original record', what could I say!

We did regular dining in nights at the Officer's Club, RAF Marham with special guests, including TV personalities Clement Freud and Lance Persival; other times I booked jazz bands such as Chris Barber and Kenny Ball. This began a bit of a working relationship with Chris Barber and we worked a number of occasions together and I got friendly with him and the band, especially drummer Graham Burbidge who was one of my original drum heroes.

Mike Donald left the band at the end of the year; I decided not to replace him and carried on till spring 1973, when I decided to finish Rick Keen. It was time for a change, I was still suffering from the after effects of my accident, both physically and what would be called today 'post traumatic stress'

I decided to freelance for the rest of the year; I'd put a band together, just for the challenge sometimes, plus other work with various musicians and line-ups. I played some trad-jazz nights at a few local pubs, which were fun and undemanding. Among the many musicians that passed through our bunch of jazzer's were Norman Potts

(Ray's father) on trumpet, Garth Coles (sax), a great trombonist who worked for the local Council, whose name I've lost in the myths of time, Ray Potts and Tony Pull (guitars), various bass players including Barry Dean when he had free time from working with Brian Auger. Roy Bentley and George McKay (Saxes) also joined the throng from time to time, as I seem to remember.

In 1973 Mike Williamson was the local Musicians Union rep and he had the chance to bring a musicians workshop to King's Lynn funded by the Musicians Union. The venue chosen was the Fairstead Pub, at the time a very respectable music venue. The late Versay Craske was the landlord through the 1970's and early 1980's and a variety of bands could be seen there up to six nights a week, with the pub always packed out. In fact, Malcolm Powell (Lynn News editor) and I once judged a talent contest at the pub!

I helped Mike organise the event, the line up was to be the great Graham Bond (keyboards). Bond of course had been a founder member of his own Graham Bond Organisation, which introduced the world to Ginger Baker, Jack Bruce, Jon Hiseman and John McLaughlin. Part of Vinegar Joe, including David Brooks (Elkie Brooks brother) came, and also Ollie Halsall from Patto's band, it was a fantastic night of music.

Bond was a strange guy, very much into the occult and along with the late Viv Stanshall, were two of the strangest people I have ever met. We all went back to Jackie Curran's house afterwards for a party that lasted till nearly dawn and my last memory of Graham was of him wandering outside, not having a clue where he was, completely out of it and trying to get into the van for the trip back to London. Still in his odd lucid moments during the evening, he was fascinating character and a much misunderstood and under appreciated musician. In less than a year he was to die in mysterious circumstances, falling under a tube train at Finsbury Park station.

Mike Williamson and I got some holiday season work as a duo at Hemsby, Hunstanton and Heacham. Working with Mike was always an unforgettable experience, his black humour knew no bounds and anyone be it audience or club bosses could soon become a figure of amusement to Mike, and how he got out of being flattened, or being banned from places is unbelievable.

I could almost write a separate book on Williamson humour, but I will reveal a couple of amusing incidents, amusing to us anyway. We were working a Gt Yarmouth holiday 'emporium' on one occasion. As with a lot of these clubs we had to amuse the kids for the first hour, before they were banned from the dance floor. We would organise games and dance competitions etc. On this particular evening not a single kid would do anything, exasperated Mike asked them to form a line down the centre of the room, a big prize was promised. At last we got a response, and with the line formed, Mike proceeded to give out instructions, which was *'to proceed out of the building through the front gates, turn left towards the roundabout, take the A47 road for 100 yards, lie down in a row and wait for the first lorry to come'*. This was not appreciated by most of their mothers, but I did catch an odd father with a smile on his face!

The Searle family (where we often played at their Holiday Village clubhouse) were often the butt of Mike's humour and often fell foul to his wit. Willie Searle ran the boat trips out of Hunstanton to view the seals on the sandbanks of the Wash, and would ask Mike to announce these trips for interested holidaymakers, this was a fatal mistake and Willie never learnt. Mike's big build up to promote Willie's excursions would go something like this *'Ladies and Gentleman, William Searle's boating experiences are once again running their popular trips to view the seals on Seal*

Island. I say once again as the last trip has only just got back from a visit last week when the boat sunk and three people are still missing, fortunately everyone else on board managed to swim to Seal Island. Richard Searle has only just missed his brother, as he rarely works, so they were only rescued today! If you still fancy a trip Willie is standing at the bar (he's the one with the seaweed in his hair) with Richard who will buy everyone in the club a drink'

Another bizarre incident happened at Heacham during a lunchtime gig. We had almost completed a spot for the kids, who had all been enthusiastic and had joined in everything we had thrown at them, except for one little boy right at the bottom of the room, who had remained seated the whole time. Latching onto this Mike cajoled him *'To get up and not be such a spoil sport'*, when this failed, and there was no such word in Mike's book, he gathered up all the children and sent them down to drag him on the floor, when this also failed, Mike got them to form a circle around the table the little boy was sitting and jeer as only children can do to another child, calling him everything they could think of, to try and get him to join in. With the complete failure of this, Mike did call it a day and thought no more of it. When we took a break the entire child's family stormed on Mike accusing him of being a cruel and callous son of a bitch, apparently the child unbeknown to us was confined to a wheel chair, which we couldn't see from the stage and of course couldn't move. Why someone hadn't come up and explained the situation before all hell let loose, we shall never know; it was the first and only time I have ever seen Mike almost lost for words! In the end he could only mutter *'I'm so sorry, how was I to know? I didn't know he was in a wheelchair'* It was like a scene from a Monty Python movie, with Mike almost getting a pint of beer thrown over him, but underneath Mike's bravado there was a kind and generous person and I know he felt very upset and sorry for the little boy.

In October I had the opportunity to fulfil a dream and visited America for the first time. Travelling from east to west, in three and a half weeks I took in New York, Washington DC, San Francisco, Los Angeles and Las Vegas. An English guy in America, even in 1973 was not that a familiar sighting and everywhere I went I met great people, saw some wonderful bands and bought my first record in years, a copy of the Allman Brothers 'Brothers and Sisters'. America lived up to all my expectations and I have returned many times over the years.

Fuelled with new ideas on my return, I got together a couple of part time bands, a rock unit I named the Tulsa City Rock Co, with Mike Donald on bass, and guitarists Ray Potts and John Worfolk. The second band was a country band I called Rockytop, with Ray and Mike, plus steel guitarist Les Wright. Neither of these bands lasted beyond a few gigs, but again it was a fun thing to do.

In early 1974 I hooked up with Ray Potts and 'Mo' Pegg to do a series of one off gigs. This was the first time in ten years I had worked with 'Mo', although we had kept in touch. These went off okay, so we decided to put something more permanent together. Ray was unavailable full time, so we roped in Mike Williamson and then added Dave Raines on keyboards (Dave is the brother of Strollers drummer Nigel). For no particular reason we called the band the Simon Grant Sound, it was mostly a top forty/dance band, and it was to last until the end of 1976 and proved to be a popular band. When later on 'Mo' decided to leave to open a shop in North Lopham, near Diss, we replaced him with Pete Carter.

One gig I remember well was backing Britain's first guitar hero Bert Weedon of *Guitar Boogie Shuffle* fame. We met up with him an hour before the start time, he gave us a list of numbers and the key they were in, and off we went. He seemed quite pleased with the results; we got paid so he must have liked us! Another time we backed comedian/singer Mike Reid, also later an 'Eastenders' actor, he was fun to work with, treated us well and shared some humorous stories about his life and career. This was a different experience to working with some of the cabaret acts booked at Hunstanton's Country Club, most of which were second-rate prima donnas with an attitude problem. We had the misfortune to be asked to back an opera singer once, which ended in chaos, when she stormed off stage because the audience wouldn't keep quiet and we hadn't a clue what she was doing. When a quality cabaret act appeared it made up for all those dreadful Tom Jones and Neil Diamond impersonators and Eddie Kidd did land some well known stars from time to time!

I still did the odd night with my dad's band; he was now in his sixties and was working a trio with Bertha Thrower on piano/keyboards, with a succession of different drummers. Bertha is a talented pianist and has been a good family friend over the years, and at 96 years, is still going strong. Mike and I worked our summer season around Great Yarmouth, Hemsby, Hunstanton and Heacham, sometimes as a duo, or as a trio with Pete Carter. At the busiest holiday period we would often be working up to ten gigs a week (7 nights plus 3 lunchtimes).

1975 would follow the same pattern although we dropped the holiday season that year. As 1976 loomed, little had changed. In the spring Carl Croucher at the Manor Park Holiday Park, Hunstanton, asked me to help him organise all the entertainment for the forthcoming holiday season. So I spent quite a bit of time there working in various formats including organists Charlie Horrex and Nick Carter, as well as duos, trios with Mike and the full band.

I met up with a number of interesting characters that summer, including a young Thalidomide victim Terry Wiles, who was having his first real holiday. Terry was a live wire and never let his disabilities get in the way of him enjoying life to the full. He loved to sing and would get alongside the band and sing several songs every time we were there. His father Len had built this amazing wheelchair that could do just about anything, and I think Terry still holds the record for the fastest 0 to 60 in a wheelchair! He later drew the attention of the 'Sunday Times' who wrote about his amazing courage, this was later turned into a successful book 'On Giants Shoulders', and a BBC2 feature length film with Terry playing himself. He went to University in America and there were several follow up programmes about his life.

Another interesting thing I did that year (or it might have been 1975) was for the King's Lynn Festival; they were just beginning to develop a fringe event to run alongside the main festival. (This would later develop into Festival Too) Fred Calvert was behind the idea to present the musical 'Joseph & The Amazing Technicolor Dreamcoat', and take it around the town using a large articulated trailer as the stage. Fred had been head of King's Lynn Police and was well known for his love of theatre and the arts, producing and appearing in several productions for the local Amateur & Dramatic Society; he possessed a rich and cultured voice and was a much admired local celebrity. He asked Ray Potts, Mike Donald and I to get together with pianist Dorothy MacDonald, as musical director, to provide the music for the local actors, singers and dancers. It all went off very well and working with Fred was a memorable happening, he treated his 'rock musicians' very well and organised a big thank you party with the Mayor in the Mayors Parlour later that year.

In the summer I first met up with two young music enthusiasts, Dick Atkinson and Colin Bailey, a friendship that has lasted through the years. Dick at the time worked for a Building Society and Colin was just starting out as a local solicitor. They introduced me to all these singer/songwriters and bands that I knew so little about, such as Randy Newman, Ry Cooder, Tom Waits and Little Feat, I could see that I had a lot of catching up to do!

I'd been too busy doing my own thing that up to 1974, I had rarely bought any records since the mid 60's, other than James Taylor, Carole King, Allman Brothers, Joe Cocker and a couple of Buddy Rich, but between '74 and '76 I developed a love for what was called jazz fusion after seeing Chick Corea's Return To Forever. I quickly moved through Miles Davis, Herbie Hancock's Headhunters, John McLaughlin's Mahavishnu Orchestra, Weather Report and Santana. I loved all the high energy that I thought was missing from a lot of post Hendrix/Cream bands and the complex rhythms of the drums and percussion soon became a new source of inspiration which I will explain more, later on.

So on a regular basis Dick, Col and I would hook up and indulge our musical inspirations and listen to tons of music, washed down equally with a large quantity of beer! A habit we still carry on to this day I'm pleased to say. They changed a lot of my opinions on music and boasted my record collection somewhat! I love these guys! And value their musical knowledge second to none.

'Mo' Pegg phoned me in the early autumn with the news that B J Wilson (Procol Harum's drummer) had just bought a house in North Lopham and been into' Mo's' shop. He mentioned me to him and said I knew him from his Paramount days with Garry Brooker, with this Barrie gave Mo his phone number and told me to get in touch. I phoned him and went over to visit the following week. Barrie and Sue Wilson had bought this large country house in the middle of the village; it was a beautiful house, completely private with a high wall surrounding the property, set in large grounds with a paddock at the rear. There was a lovely old barn, which Barrie renovated and built his recording studio and games room, complete with jukebox and snooker table.

Sue and Barrie made me welcome and we developed a lasting friendship and I spent many happy days at Lopham. Barrie had just returned from Miami where Procul had recorded an album, released in 1977 called 'Something Magic'.

Barrie like me had an inherent love of percussion and had a great collection of cowbells, wood blocks, ago-go bells, bongos, timbales etc, in fact anything that would make a noise! I use to take my kit over and we'd spend a day swapping ideas and jamming away. Barrie had for a long time been one of my favourite British rock drummers. Procul were a very innovative band and I had always loved his fabulous drumming, he had a formidable style, which bore more resemblance to American second-line rhythms, such as Little Feat's Ritchie Hayward than say the more straight ahead Keith Moon British style.

Born in 1947, he joined the Paramounts when only 16 years. In early 1967 Gary Brooker had his first idea for what was to become Procol Harum. Barrie was there at this early stage, but dropped out, only to rejoin later in the year on the strength of Procul's surprise massive hit *Whiter Shade Of Pale*. Ten years with Procul and ten huge selling albums, they toured the world and became one of the most talked about band of the 60/70's.

Barrie had also played with Jimmy Page on Joe Cocker's debut album that resulted in the huge hit single *With A Little Help From My Friends* pinned down by Barrie's distinctive tom-toms patterns and three-quarter time beat. I think his drumming on this song was so innovative, and really defined his signature drum sound. There are various stories as to how the band came up with the idea of transforming the original Beatles version into a rock waltz, but Barrie later told me, that he and Jimmy Page started to jam the song and had started to put a three-quarter beat into it, that led to those famous tom tom sounds.

In late 1976 Pete Carter and I decided to have one last stab at forming a new rock band. We recruited talented Simon Lilley on guitar, originally from Brighton he was looking for work after working on the Mecca circuit and ending up in King's Lynn. In early 1977 we set about rehearsals, putting together a set list and stage show. In the meantime to get things off the ground and keep earning a living, we also decided to do some regular trio work.

We picked what now sounds a ridiculous name Goldyrocks, we rehearsed a set list, got photos and publicity printed and bombarded the agents from far afield, which resulted in nothing, in fact 'zilch', not to be deterred we carried on still hoping our luck would change. To get the sound I wanted, I changed my usual Ludwig kit for a larger Ludwig in matt black, it had a 24inch bass drum that produced a wonderful 'thwack', I loved playing that kit. As the summer neared we were finding it difficult to get work, so to get us by we took a season job at a holiday village in Skegness. This proved to be a fatal mistake, it was horrendous, the clubhouse seemed to be packed each week with drunken miners from the Midlands and North of England, and they all had their designated holiday weeks. All they were interested in was getting drunk as quickly as possible, leaving their children to run riot, leaping across the stage knocking everything over and nobody cared. The management of the club never did spell the band name correctly, that hardly mattered, as music was low on the list of priorities. We were all affected in one way or another, Simon who always loved a drink, became a professional alcoholic, Pete never wanted to see the inside of a holiday park again. and I was at near breaking point, on anti-depressants and didn't play drums again for several months. The band split up, but not before we were bestowed the honour of playing before the Duke of Kent and his family at a special occasion to mark the silver anniversary to commemorate the Queen's succession, which was held at Park House, Sandringham. We cancelled what little work we had and I have never been near Skegness again. The whole episode only emphasised the vast difference that exists between being a kind of circus clown entertainer, and a musician playing music to entertain and hopefully being appreciated for his talent. But in some ways, I'm glad this happened because it made me rethink my life and career. Since my accident I'd tried to live life to the full, not wanting to miss a minute and I was acutely aware how life could be snapped away in an instance. I'd rebelled and partied to the full, not that I was about to change everything, but nonetheless I had to re-evaluate what I was going to do in the future and in the year ahead I would try to make some changes.

I realised music was becoming 'as serious as my life', if you let it happen music can turn negative and drag you down with it, so I had to take the positive vibes out of music and only concentrate on that aspect. I sold my Ludwig to a fellow drummer and bought a small Gretsch jazz kit, I added a percussion tree with lots of 'toys', plus other cowbells and cymbals and practised a style of playing both drums and percussion at the same time. I would use this to great advantage in the years ahead; it provided a fuller sound that made up for the lack of 'foot power' that over the time ahead would further decline, as each year passed.

Barrie Wilson was at a loose end after Procul had split earlier in the year and had joined the Frankie Miller Band to tour, and record Miller's album 'Double Trouble'. He was doing a gig at the old Rainbow, Finsbury Park and invited me along. I took Mike Williamson and it was a great night of music. The band was smokin' complete with a hot horn section with Paul Carrick on keyboards, we went to the party afterwards and got to meet a few famous people and of course joined in the hospitality offered.

In May 1978 I joined the James Elliot Band with singer Kevin Dagg, who as Larry Bond had fronted the 60's band the Strangers. Also in the band was George McKay (saxes, flute), with Tim Nesbitt (bass) and Harry Brien (guitar). During the next eighteen months the band existed, Pete Carter replaced Tim and Ronnie Pitt took over on guitar from Harry. Kevin also left later on to work in the Middle East, so there were quite a few changes. It was a good band and we were able to play pretty much what we wanted, and any band that included George would always be enjoyable. George, Pete and I went on to work together in several jazz configurations, the first of which was 52nd Street, a be-bop style band formed by tenor sax player Roy Bentley. We played the Castle Hotel, Downham Market and built up quite a following, this led to some work at the Riverside Restaurant, King's Lynn (part of the Guildhall, King's Lynn), including a session for the King's Lynn Festival. Roy also taught music in schools, so we also did a few school workshops which were fun. Roy was a talented musician who had moved to Norfolk from London, he knew most of the London jazz fraternity and had a passion for Charlie Parker.

I went to the Nice Jazz Festival on the French Rivera in July, and would return a few more times over the coming years. It was held in this Roman amphitheatre high above the town, it wasn't just jazz, blues and roots type bands were also on the programme. I saw Professor Longhair and the great James Booker, as well as Dizzy Gillespie and Stan Getz, who despite his reputation as a difficult individual I was able to spend ten minutes chatting to him about his music and the fact he was one of my first jazz heroes. I also met up with two fellow musicians from Manchester, drummer Ken Leyland and keyboardist John Rodway, over the years they became close friends and we met up regularly at Nice and the North Sea Festival in Holland and we still catch up from time to time to share our jazz interests.

My old friend Bob Booth who a decade earlier had brought to King's Lynn the supergroup ESP, decided it was time to stun music fans once more and present a star-studded rock evening at the Tech in King's Lynn (now the College Of West Anglia). So we put together a band just for one night, Bob wanted to feature drummers so we roped in Nigel Portass and I invited Barrie over as special name guest and all three of us featured in a drum solo special as the climax of the show. Despite being packed out I don't think many realised they had witnessed the great B J Wilson in action.

Dick Atkinson had moved to a village near to Barrie and I'd introduced them earlier in the year and before Sue and Barrie moved to America in late 1978, we used to spend some riotous evenings together from what I can remember!

I had long thought about looking for a part time job of some kind, partly to have some extra income coming in, but also to get me away from music 24/7. I was now 35 years old and knew I would be very lucky to still keep making enough money purely from music, but because the injuries in the accident had left me unable to stand for long periods and tire easily, any job would be potentially difficult. I also had to manage constant pain of variable degree which also didn't help. In October I saw a job advertised for a part time sales negotiator for Barratt Housebuilders, hours 11.00am to 6.00pm, two days a week. I phoned and got an interview. I was offered the job and I began a career in property that spanned over twenty years and in time would become fulltime. I eventually went on to become a Sales Office Manager as well as diversifying for a while as a Land Buyer and Land Researcher. It was the only other form of work I could cope with, really enjoyed and was successful at.

Local drummer and author of drum tutors; John Savage opened up a music shop and began having evening drum workshops. Jon Hiseman and Peter York were among the many drummers that came and I also remember Paiste cymbals did a promotional evening where I got to try a whole rackful of cymbals. When I went to London to a Billy Cobham drum clinic sometime later in that year, Jon Hiseman and the guy from Paiste were waiting in the queue, they remembered me and invited me join them and we got to spend some time with Cobham talking about his innovative drumming and career.

As I mentioned earlier I got very interested in Latin style percussion that I could equally infuse with both rock and jazz. I developed this cross hand method of playing percussion, cymbals etc with my left hand while playing snare drum and hi-hat with my right, and with George McKay I got really into this.

Over the next two or three years George put together an assortment of jazz groups from straight jazz, jazz rock, fusion and Latin and I got the opportunity to play with a lot of different musicians, so many, I can't remember them all. I was able to document my playing at that time and have a live recording Live At The Cross Keys, that Nigel Portass set up that featured Nigel (keyboards), Pete Carter (bass), George (saxes/flute/congas) and me, and I'm quite proud of my playing on this. We didn't rehearse anything, but apart from a few mistakes it turned out pretty good. George often got some London guys down to join us at our regular haunts at the old Rummer pub in King's Lynn and the long lost Ingoldisthorpe Manor Hotel. One night he brought along this extraordinary sax player who turned out to be the legendary Mike Osborne, as well known as Tubby Hayes and Ronnie Scott on the 60's London jazz scene. I continued to spend time with Barrie and we got together to play drums as often as time permitted, I learned a lot from him and he was a constant inspiration in all my playing, but I was equally flattered when Barrie would quiz me on some of the things I was doing. With the studio now up and running we would often put down some stuff, this later led to me taking Pete over to record some tracks for real. Pete had got heavily into playing sitar after seeing Indian fusion band Shakti back in 1976, so we worked out some songs overdubbing Pete on sitar and bass, with Barrie on tablas, bells and other assorted percussion and myself on congas, bongos, cymbals, cowbells etc. This music was what would be called World Music today, and we put several hours into getting everything sounding right. The idea was to try and get this commercially released at sometime, but unfortunately we never got round to getting this off the ground. Sue still has these tapes that became known as the 'Barn Tapes and we talked about them when I last visited her.

In May 1979 we took the children to Disney World in Florida, it was good to get to spend time with them and like all children they lapped up the fantasy world that Disney offers and I have happy memories of this time.

I kept in contact with Sue and Barrie after they relocated to America and they had started to build a house in rural Oregon; Barrie had a lot of contacts in America, particularly in Los Angeles and had been promised some studio and touring work.

I continued with James Elliot, but by the end of the year we were all getting a little fed up with the general band scene and being treated as second class citizens at some of the venues we played at. We split up on New Years Eve after watching everyone there tucking into chicken, chips and desserts and only being offered one small plate of chicken to share between the four of us, because they had forgotten the band! (the story of my life), so the 80's beckoned, a decade that brought many changes in my life and what would become the last real period of my musical career.

Chapter Eleven – Still Rockin' After All These Years (The 1980's & Beyond)

The start of the 80's found me once again wondering which musical direction to take. As the year progressed I would find that direction, but for now I continued with some freelance work and took up an offer from Mike Williamson to work some trio gigs with the late Aubrey Harrod (tenor sax & vocals). Aubrey was a lovely guy and a good musician and had been in several local bands over the years, but this was the first opportunity I had had to work with him. I worked on and off with Mike and Aubrey for the rest of the year, it was enjoyable, but I really wanted to get back into something more musically challenging.
As the middle of the year approached I got word that Al Drake wanted to reorganise Good News, the band he and his wife Maureen (Mo) had been running for the past two or three years with drummer Dennis Scott and ex-Tea Time Four bassist John Cork. Pete Carter came to see me and we went to see Al to talk about the possibilities. Mo was a hell of a singer with a dynamic stage presence and Al wanted to capitalize more on her sheer talent and build a band around her, that would be able to reproduce chart songs quickly, as well as playing a wide range of other popular material. Al proposed to wind his old band up at the end of the year and to start the new one at the beginning of 1981. Pete and I were interested straight away; after all we had been in bands on and off together for what seemed like eternity, although I hadn't gigged with Al for almost ten years. We both agreed to join Mo and Al and looked forward to starting this new venture at the beginning of 1981. It was to be the musical challenge I was looking for and it would be almost a decade of hard drinking, some great music, as well as some personal ups and downs.
Sue and Barrie invited me over to Oregon in the early autumn and I first spent a little time in Seattle to see the stunning mountain scenery, before heading down to Portland. Sue and Barrie had built a lovely house on land that Sue's parents owned in the Kings Valley area of central Oregon, it was a beautiful, remote location and completely secluded and very green!
Since living in America Barrie had secured some LA studio dates, appearing on several tracks of the debut John Hiatt album 'Slug Line' as well as recording with Tom Petty. In 1979 he once again hooked up with old friend Joe Cocker, who at the time was living down the coast in the mountains above Santa Barbara California, in a house he rented from Jane Fonda. Barrie joined Joe's band for the tenth anniversary Woodstock tour that original joint Woodstock promoter Michael Lang had organised. Fuelled by the success of this tour, Joe was on a roll and formed a new band that included Barrie. Michael Lang would soon take over as Joe's manager, which led him having a massive joint hit in 1982 with Jennifer Warnes. taking *Up Where We Belong* from the movie 'An Officer & A Gentleman' into the top ten. Barrie was to remain with Joe until 1984, a fabulous live album 'Live In New York' was recorded at a concert in Central Park in July 1980, which documents the band at their height and bares witness just how good Joe could be with the right musicians backing him.
With Sue and Barrie I spent time exploring the Oregon countryside and the breathtaking coastline of the Pacific Northwest. After leaving Oregon I travelled down the west coast stopping off in LA, San Diego and ending up in Tijuana, Mexico, before returning to England in late November.

No sooner had I got back than 'Henry' my faithful friend for almost thirteen years was taken ill, I took him to the vet, but alas I had to have him put to sleep, there would be no more wagging tale when I arrived home at 3.00am.

In January 1981 I got together with Al, Mo and Pete and we launched what was to be known as Maureen & The Three Piece Sweet. We decided to rehash the old band name and this began the longest period I ever worked in the same band, a span that lasted from January 1981 to October 1990. We knew right from the start what we wanted from this band, we didn't want to travel long distances and intended to 'cherry pick' our gigs. This may sound arrogant, but we were all a little older, but not necessarily wiser and wanted this band to be as hassle free as possible.

The band mixed top forty hits with old rock 'n' roll, a touch of country and some standards, a formula that we stuck to all the way through the life of the band. It worked and we became hugely popular throughout the 80's and for the most part it was enjoyable, and Mo's version of the Elkie Brooks hit *Pearl's A Singer* would always bring the audience to their feet in rapturous applaud!

When time permitted, I also started to do a few gigs with local clarinettist Dave Baker's Jazzcats. It was a 'good time' fun band and among the many gigs was a regular spot at Burnham Market's Hoste Arms, this was long before becoming the celebrity hangout of today (no Stephen Fry's back then) and the pub would always be packed out with a wide age range of music lovers. Dave's band had an ever revolving personnel and I worked on and off with him until about 1984. Dave was originally from London, settling in the King's Lynn area in the mid 70's, he was a colourful character and built up a large following with the various band line-ups he put together. In 1984, when Barrie was staying with me for a couple of days, I took him along to a gig I had with Dave at the Riverside Restaurant gardens, and he got up and played a couple of numbers with the band, and really enjoyed it!

Mo and I soon built up a great working relationship and friendship and shared the same zany humour. Mo and Al would usually rehearse the majority of new material first, with Pete and me coming in later for the final rehearsals, this worked out well and we could always keep up to date with new chart songs quickly. Mo was featured vocalist on the majority of the set list, with Al and Pete sharing lead vocals on other songs, as well as joining Mo on backing vocals.

Life on the road was never short of a few laughs; Mo could (and often did) drink anyone under the table! I remember on one occasion when she decided to cut back, just a little on her drinking and brought along a three litre carton of wine to last through the weekend gigs, however this only lasted the first night, which was typical Mo! We got to know Helena and Barry Anderson very well when they managed the former Hotel Mildenhall in King's Lynn, and the band worked there regularly during the 80's. This work included the many Christmas parties that were held during the run up to the festive season and we would set up our gear at the beginning of December and leave it there for most of the month. At other times during the year we would be booked for various functions and it became a home from home for us.

Barry is a Geordie and has this unbelievable accent and when he has downed a couple of drinks, becomes almost incoherent and his Christmas party speeches were not to be missed. Helena's mother is Peggy Spencer the ballroom dancing star of BBC TV's 'Come Dancing'; Peggy was often at the hotel and now lives in King's Lynn.

As I said earlier, there were plenty of laughs with the band and I remember a couple of amusing incidents, both of which happened at the Hotel Mildenhall. We were booked to play for a wedding anniversary or birthday, and during the evening Helena came up to the stage with this beautiful cake to present to the lady, on her special day.

Al got the lady on stage and Helena passed the cake to Mo to do the honours (probably a mistake as Mo had downed a few that evening) and without batting an eyelid, she pushed the cake into the lady's face and with soft icing and cream streaming down her face and dress, Mo was heard to utter 'I've always wanted to do that'.

Often there would be several smaller parties booked for the same evening. On one of these occasions a young guy was there with friends to celebrate his eighteenth birthday. They had booked a surprise birthday 'stripergram' which the hotel readily agreed to, but nobody was prepared for what was to happen next. The beautiful young girl duly arrived with her minder, who set up her backing tapes and placed a chair centre room, when the time came she went over and led the somewhat surprised youth over to the chair, sat him down and began a very slow and seductive strip in front of him, ending up completely naked and then to the gasps of the audience proceeded to liberally spread cream on various parts of her body and got the 'birthday boy' to lick this off leaving nothing to the imagination (I will spare you the intimate details). This caused a near riot in the room as the audience split into those that thought Christmas had arrived early, who were cheering loudly and loving every minute, with the remaining audience looking on horrified and disgusted. One man was cheering and trying to get a better view, only to have a pint of beer poured over him by his not so enthusiastic girlfriend, others were dragged away by their partners protesting loudly, glasses were thrown and it took poor Helena the rest of the evening to calm and apologise to her not so understanding customers. As for the band, we all agreed it was one of the most memorable evenings we had ever spent at the Mildenhall!

I know I can appear an arrogant and a stubborn sod at times, but I'm usually a very calm and laid back type of guy and I don't lose my cool too easily unless provoked, but like most people there is a breaking point. So Mo would look forward to my occasional explosions, that she would describe as Dick's 'twice yearly, completely losing it' situations'. I once narrowly avoided a disastrous eruption which had developed when someone had taken a disliking to the hat I was wearing, which in no time had escalated into a near fracas until someone stepped in to calm us down.

In October 1982 Barrie was in Europe on tour with Joe Cocker and he invited me to London, where the band was appearing at the former Hammersmith Odeon. We met up at the Hilton, early afternoon. By the end of the afternoon an assortment of guests had arrived, including the eccentric late Viv Stanshall (of Bonzo Dog fame) who swept into the Hilton wearing plus-fours and a long flowing cape! Barrie's old mates from Procol, Garry Brooker, Keith Reid and Procol's producer Chris Thomas were also there (Chris is a noted session player and producer, who worked with George Martin on The Beatles 'White Album', he also produced albums for Elton John). Dick Atkinson came along and Barrie took us to meet Joe in the bar where we proceeded to down a few pints and chat about the good 'ole days, before we all got on the band coach to take us to the Odeon. Joe's Mum, Madge joined us on the bus, she was a wonderful lady, and I have a photograph of Joe that she gave me that evening. Joe's manager Michael Lang greeted us back stage and we had our 'access all areas' badges. It was a great night of music; Joe was magic and one of the all time greats. The band just tore up the place with Barrie playing a dream. A few old friends of Joe's turned up in the dressing room after the gig, including fellow singer Chris Farlowe. Back at the hotel we took over the bar where Joe got the resident pianist to play some blues, and he sang a few songs. I chatted to the surreal Viv Stanshall and I recall the first words he said to me 'Are they your real teeth?'

It was a memorable evening and having the opportunity to hang out with Joe was something I shall always remember.

With all the touring out of L.A. in the early 80's, Sue and Barrie rented a house down in Ventura California, and I went over in the summer of 1983 to see them. It's a great part of the world with Malibu on one side and Santa Barbara on the other. I caught up with Joe once more and Barrie took me to a great jazz club overlooking the beach in Malibu, where we sampled a few too many 'cocktails' and unfortunately made rather a mess of the inside of Sue's car!

July 1985 found me back at the Nice Jazz Festival and I hooked up with some French fans who gladly shared their 'wine and weed'. Chuck Berry was just one of the many musicians appearing that year. Other included Miles Davis, Lee Ritenour, Steps Ahead, B.B King, and Flora Purim. Nice was always a good place to hang out with its friendly and relaxed atmosphere and an opportunity to meet and chat to the many famous musicians that played there.

In late 1985 my grandmother, my number one fan died aged 104 years, this was not perhaps entirely unexpected, but up to that time she had been in reasonable health for her years. I still miss her very much today, for her words of wisdom and her unstoppable enthusiasm, and love of life.

Not long after the funeral my marriage completely fell apart, Maggie walked out and never returned. I'd always done my best to hold everything together, but in reality our marriage had been hitting the rocks for several years. Nevertheless at the time this was a tremendous shock and came right out of the blue. Nick and Rae were to remain with me and we somehow got through Christmas. Not long into the New Year, Maggie moved in with Pete Carter, this of course caused a major problem both personally and professionally and I took it badly. Pete immediately quit the band and this ended our friendship and musical partnership.

The next couple of years or so were difficult; I began drinking more and juggling prescription pills. After the divorce Pete and Maggie married and I didn't see much of them for several years, but time has healed certain old wounds and we do occasionally meet up, particularly for family occasions now we have lots of grandchildren growing up.

I was now working full time selling houses and soon found dividing the time between my day job, the band, cooking, cleaning and looking after two teenage children hard going, to say the least. Al and Mo were very supportive to me at this time and were always there to pick me up during the lows.

We decided to carry on with the band and replaced Pete with Graham Ball, who although thrown in at the deep end, soon adapted to the difficult role of replacing Pete Carter.

I managed to get Nick to Middlesex University in 1986; meanwhile Rae continued with her education before taking a job in King's Lynn and eventually moving away from the area and getting married.

After visiting Nice in 1986 I flew on to America and spent some time with Sue and Barrie. He was feeling a little depressed after losing the drum chair in Joe's band, after he had reformed the band line up. Being up in Oregon and away from the LA scene meant Barrie was losing touch with his many contacts, however he was reasonably optimistic that something would turn up soon and we hung out and had fun drinking Jim Beam and sharing the local 'home grown' herbal products.

In September 1987 at a time when I was feeling particularly down, I bumped into Chrissie who quite literally turned my life around. My children knew Chrissie, and were friends with her son Rick. In Chrissie I found a soul mate that believed in me and understood my eccentric personality. I also gained Rick who has become a good friend and like a second son to me. I owe a great deal to her for her love and support over the years. We set up home together the following year, we have shared our love for travel, and she even likes some of my music!

Not long after I met Chrissie I received the devastating news that Barrie was in a coma and on a life support system after a tragic accident. He was to remain in a coma until 1990 when he died peacefully in hospital. I had lost a great friend and as someone once described Barrie, he was both 'a gentle man and a gentleman'. Over the years we had shared some great times together and I valued his friendship greatly. It was a sad time for family and friends, particularly Sue and their children Sarah and Nicola. Barrie always put his music and loyalty first over money and gain, turning down offers to join Led Zeppelin while with Procol and then famously turning down Paul McCartney to join Wings, because he didn't want McCartney telling him how to play the drums. I will never forget him.

In October 1990 we decided to disband and played our last gig as Maureen & The Three Piece Sweet at St Margaret's Club, King's Lynn. It was completely packed out and owner Alan Holden presented us with silver tankards to commemorate the evening, it was the end of an era.

After almost ten years with the band it was time to take a break and I didn't pick up a drum stick again for a long, long time, and then only on an odd occasion when my old friend Graham Ball persuaded me to join him and guitarists Eddie Reed and Phil Warnes for the occasional evening playing just for fun in local pubs.

I thoroughly enjoyed these intermittent gigs and felt I'd completed a full circle, once again playing a mixture of roots, blues and rock as I'd more or less started out with way back in 1962. Importantly for me the music we played was always of the highest quality and I had finally mastered that laid back 'second line' feel. I owe a big 'thank you' to Graham, Eddie and Phil for making me go out and play, allowing me to bow out on a high note!

I really didn't miss playing drums on a regular basis; I was now living a somewhat quieter, slower and more sober lifestyle. Although I had been involved with the music business for well over thirty five years; it had never really been for the glory, but because I loved creating music. Unfortunately the first signs of arthritis were showing and I needed a rest, it would have been impossible for me to have tried to continue as before, and in the end I had to quit completely, due to my arthritic and worsening leg problems and my drums are now long gone. I continued with my day job until this health problem compounded and I was forced into taking early medical retirement and now walk with the aid of sticks with my mobility restricted.

Looking back over my long and varied career in music, I feel I have been extraordinarily lucky and privileged to have to have been part of history in the making with my involvement with the Hamburg music era. I don't think the Sabres received the full recognition they deserved and sadly our good luck ran out before the potential of the band could be fully appreciated by a far wider audience, but hey! that's life and I have no regrets. I may not have become a 'star', but I was able to pursue a multi directional musical career and I think I did pretty well and achieved many musical goals. The memories of those 'Hamburg Days' will remain with me forever and it's been a lifetime journey taking me from the 'Maids Head to Hamburg' and way beyond that!

Chapter Twelve – Bringing The Music Up To Date (1992 – 2006))

My dad died quite suddenly in 1992, just short of his 80th birthday. After much persuasion by Chrissie he had just started to play his violin again and had been busy putting together a programme of his favourite songs that he was going to perform with Bertha Thrower on his birthday. Sadly this was not to be, we still have his song list that he was going to play, something we shall always treasure. After a short illness my mum died in 1999, but she did live long enough to see three great-grandchildren that she was very proud of.

Losing my parents left a huge void in my life and I miss them both immensely, and with no other close relatives the only child syndrome hit home, but of course we have our children and grandchildren, lots of them! As an only child it seems strange at times to have such a large and ever expanding family.

We are very proud of them all; Nick went into teaching and was a Housemaster at a school in the West Midlands, before moving to Wales where he is now Head of Geography at a public school in Monmouth. Married with three children he is kept pretty busy. Rae has now completed a three year training course and is a Staff Nurse at Queen Elizabeth Hospital in King's Lynn. She has married for the second time and now has three children; and still lives in West Norfolk. Rick is the computer wizard in the family and is married with a young son, after living in Sussex for a while he and his family are now settled in Hertfordshire.

I started to seriously get into collecting and researching American music in the early 90's and now have a large collection of CD's, books and magazines on blues, folk, country, roots, Americana and of course jazz! I have a love for all this great music that seems never ending. I became a founder member of the now defunct 'World Jazz Network', which a guy on America's west coast started in the late 80's, and I started to contribute a few articles and reviews for their newsletter. This led me to meet some of my jazz heroes including Betty Carter, Herbie Hancock, Chick Corea, Michael Brecker, Pat Metheny and Peter Erskine.

My musings on the music scene later led me into contact with musician Marc Bristol, who together with his wife Gaby publishes the successful American rock/roots magazine 'Blue Suede News'. In one of Marc's editorials he mentioned a visit to a Hamburg bar, when he was touring Germany with his band, before coming to England to play a rock n' roll weekend at Hemsby. I e-mailed Marc mentioning my time in Hamburg, as well as my frequent gigs at Hemsby and suggested we probably had some common ground. With a bit of persuasion he asked me to write about my Hamburg experience's, which resulted in 'Hamburg Days' gracing the pages of Blue Suede News #54 (spring 2001). Marc also suggested I ought to write a book about my life as a musician as it sounded interesting, well interesting or not, here it is and it is partly due to his suggestion and the ideas and help of Kingsley Harris that my life as a musician seemed worthy of publication.

Marc later asked me to write some CD reviews for his magazine, it keeps my mind active and prevents any 'senior' moments creeping in and it's been an immensely fun thing to do from time to time, although I would never describe myself as a writer by any stretch of the imagination. I have never received payment for any of my 'writings' over the years, nor have I wanted to, but it's good to be respected for my musical knowledge and to still be involved in the music scene.

In 2003 I celebrated my 60th birthday with a journey to New York on one of the last flights of Concorde, something I had always wanted to do. It was a quick trip, but magical nonetheless. It was also a year for some reflection and a look back at my life, something I don't normally do. Some of these memories which I have written about for this book have been painful, particularly re-living my accident with such clarity and recalling the events of that October night so many years ago.

As the years have rolled away it is inevitable that you lose touch with a lot of former friends and band colleagues and sadly some are no longer with us. Al Drake suffered a stroke in 2001 that left him partly immobilised. He has now picked up the guitar again and with his son Louis's help is now making inroads into playing once more. Mo is no longer singing, but is still busy with her painting. I bump into Mike Prior from time to time; he is quite successful as a solo artist and has developed into a pretty good guitarist too! John Nockolds is still active playing guitar with various friends. I catch up with 'Mo' Pegg a couple or so times a year; he is still living in East Anglia and dabbles a bit on keyboard and guitar. After a gap of thirty years I recently caught up with Tony Relph, it was good to see him and how does he manage to look so young! Tony Pull is still in the area and playing guitar and we share some music and an occasional drink together. Mike Williamson is now living near Bristol, but we keep in regular contact and he sometimes plays guitar for some charity events. I keep in contact with my 'friendly rival' Dennis Scott and its good that he's still enthusiastic, gigging and playing great drums. John Worfolk is still active in music, doing the odd gig when he takes time off from his guitar and amp collection and his impressive juke boxes; we meet up regularly to share our mutual interest in the blues. Barry 'Fats' Dean moved to Florida, he is still very involved in the music scene, playing bass in a great blues/soul band called Blues 4 Soul, and we keep in contact from time to time. Bob Booth has now retired from his record shop, but we catch up every couple of weeks or so to discuss putting the music world to right! Sadly some old friends have died, Les Garner (aka Danny Ford) in 2004, Boz Burrell and George McKay both in 2006.

Sue Wilson, Sarah and Nicola are all still living in America; we keep in touch and visit each other when we can. I caught up with Gary Brooker a couple years or so ago when Dick Atkinson and I went to see Sarah, when she was staying with Gary and his wife Franky. Sarah lives in LA and is a successful interior designer, working for the likes of Rod Stewart and has recently married TV producer Joe Coleman, who works for US television. Nicola like her dad is into music, writing her own songs and is in a band in the San Diego area. Sue is still living in Oregon, close to where her mom, dad and other close family members live. Gary still tours occasionally with a re-vamped Procul Harum and over the years has also toured and recorded with Bill Wyman and Ringo Starr.

I have been fortunate in being able to travel to many parts of the world, not just America. Chrissie and I have been right round the world and have friends in New Zealand, Australia, Switzerland as well as America. I put my travel bug down to all those hours talking to dear Lala Bill about her world travels so many years ago!

It's strange how on our travels we have met people who have King's Lynn connections. In Indonesia we met an Australian whose son used to ride for King's Lynn Speedway. While on a stopover in Singapore we got talking to a New Zealander who once came to King's Lynn for a job interview, and staying in Hawaii we met a guy from Portland Oregon, who was taking part in the annual triathlon. He told me his first bike race had been between King's Lynn and Norwich when he visited England as a student….it's a small world!

I've bumped into some of my musical heroes in much the same way. On our way back from a visit to New Orleans where we'd seen Dr John, we stopped off in Washington DC. We stayed at a hotel just off Dupont Circle and one night at dinner I heard a familiar voice, and on turning round saw Herbie Hancock talking to Ron Carter (Herbie and Ron among other things were part of Miles Davis's famous 60's quintet). I had chance to talk to them both and asked them about working with Miles, Ron Carter wanted to know all about Hamburg. After responding it was hardly in the same league, he replied 'it's all music'.

Like everyone else I've had my share of ups and downs, but I was lucky to have had the opportunity to pursue my deep love of music in so many directions. I feel sad sometimes when I look around today and see so many talented young musicians who find it difficult to achieve their musical ambitions. Most pop music today is geared to consumer fashion and there is not much room for individualism or creative talent. To the large majority of today's young, listening to music is a background activity while playing computer games, and going to see a local band playing live is not high on their list of priorities, but I am hopeful that out of all this consumerism young bands and musicians will still find places to gig and an audience to listen to them, there are some great bands out there, go seek them out and keep supporting live music!

THANKS! (MAID'S HEAD TO HAMBURG)

When I started writing this book I had no idea how time consuming it would be and without the help of friends to jog my memory and contribute photos and additional information some of these historical ramblings may not have reached print. While I cannot guarantee a hundred per cent accuracy in all the events told I have done my best to check facts with research and information obtained. I do not take responsibility for any errors or misinformation.
There are many people to thank, not only for their contribution to this book, but also to my life as a musician.

To my fellow 60's musicians – Mike Prior, John Nockolds, Al Drake, Pete Carter, Tony Relph, Dave Stoddard, Denny Raven (aka Barry Leader), Maurice 'Mo' Pegg, Mike Williamson, Dennis Scott, Mike Donald, Roy Williamson, Rod Shirley, Tony Pull, Nigel Portass, Nick Carter, the late Paul Chris, the late Danny Ford (aka Les Garner), the late Roger Wagg, Ricky & Geoff Wilson, Larry Bond (aka Kevin Dagg), Derrick Brunton, David & Bryan Seymour, Tony Cater, Richard Sexton, Derek Stringer, Des Neville, Nigel Raines, Danny Eves, Bernie Rudd, Rocky Brown, John Cork, Barry 'Fats' Dean, the late Boz Burrell and the late Mike Patto (apologies to anyone not mentioned)

A special thanks to Mo & Al Drake, Mike Williamson, Mary Relph, Maurice 'Mo' Pegg, Dick Atkinson (for photos and providing other details etc), Colin Bailey (for all your legal advice over the years and proof reading 'Maids Head To Hamburg) and Bob Booth (for photos, help with this project etc and your expert computer guidance). You guys came up with the goods! with sincere apologies to anyone I may have inadvertently left out.

Thanks and happy memories to those who shared my 'Hamburg Days'. Peter Eckhorn, Iain Hines, Rikki Barnes, Issy Bond, the late Alex Harvey, Tony Sheridan, Pete Best, Jackie Lynton, The Searchers, Cliff Bennett & The Rebel Rousers, The Beatmen, The Blues System, The Checkmates, The Tornados, King Size Taylor, Bobby Patrick, Gigi, Ursula Voss and many, many more wherever you may be!

Thanks also to all the following – Dougie Mears, Bertha Thrower, Noel Linge, John Wickham, Jack Barrie, Colin Atkinson, George Chappell, the late George McKay, Ronnie Pitt, Simon Lilley, Ray Potts, the late Norman Potts, the late Garth Coles, Lionel Francis, the late Geoff Hopkinson, Geoff Stinton, Steve Tegg, Jackie Curran, Trevor Marriott, Mal Ashby, Les Wright, Terry Rose, Mervyn J Futter, Dave Raines, the late Frank Walton, Roy Bentley, John Savage, Dave Baker, Chris Barber, Joe Cocker, Gary Brooker, and Peter Erskine (thanks for sparing the time to talk, the CD's and your interest in my writing)

A special thanks to all the following: - Graham Ball, Eddie Reed & Phil Warnes (here's to 'Harry' lets do 'Black Magic Woman' one more time), Rose & Jack Eagle (& all the family), Ruth (& all the family), John Rodway & Ken Leyland. Peter Gathergood, Helena & Barry Anderson, Alan Holden, John Worfolk (my blues buddy), Chris Atkinson, My music sharing friends worldwide Melanie Sunbeam Smith (USA), Robere LeHuquet (USA), Bob Washington (USA), Dennis Hendley

(USA), Geoffrey Totton (New Zealand). Jan Ramsey & Joseph Irrera (Offbeat Magazine, New Orleans), Sheila (who encouraged me to play drums), Ruby (for the Escorts TV photos), to all my neighbours, (thanks for putting up with the occasional loud music) to all the many friends I made in my house selling days, both buyers and work colleagues (apologies for not naming you all) and to all my friends everywhere.

An extra big thanks to Marc Bristol & Gaby Maag-Bristol (Blue Suede News, USA) who put the idea of writing a book to me in the first place and for publishing 'Hamburg Days' (the Sabres story) and Kingsley Harris & Liz Farrow (East Anglian Music Archive) for all their input, design and help in getting this book published.

My love to Sue Wilson, Sarah, Nicola (and all the family in Oregon)

To the loving memory of my parents – Nina & Eric Meek and my grandmother Lily Williams (for giving me all your love and encouragement)

Much love to the family Nick, Jules, Rae, Paul, Rick, Donna, Josh, Beth, Elin, Harry, Owain, Ben & Dylan.

Most of all my love to Chrissie for her unwavering love, support and for putting up with me.

TOP 10 TEN LISTS (In no particular order)

Top 10 Movies

Deliverance
Spinal Tap
No Surrender
The Vanishing (original Dutch version)
Short Cuts
Leaving Las Vegas
Paris, Texas
Stealing Beauty
Tin Men
King Of Comedy

Top 10 Albums

Johnny Adams – Walking On A Tightrope
Mcoy Tyner - Sama Layuca
Astor Piazzolla – Tango Zero Hour
Joe Cocker – Live In New York
Ry Cooder – Chicken Skin Music
Weather Report – 8.30
Miles Davis – Live In Montreaux (Box Set)
Flora Purim – Stories To Tell
Little Feat – Waiting For Columbus
John McLaughlin – Heart Of Things (Live In Paris)

Top 10 Drummers

Buddy Rich
Steve Gadd
B J Wilson
Billy Cobham
Jim Keltner
Dennis Chambers
Tony Williams
Richie Hayward
Peter Erskine
Bill Stewart

Top 10 Live Concerts

Chuck Berry / Carl Perkins – (Nottingham UK, 1964)
Buddy Rich – (Ronnie Scott's, London UK, 1971)
Chick Corea's Return To Forever – (Ronnie Scott's, London UK, 1972)
Weather Report / George Duke & Billy Cobham Band / John McLaughlin's Shakti –
                      (Hammersmith Odeon, London UK, 1976)
Joe Cocker – (Hammersmith Odeon, London UK, 1982

Miles Davis – (Nice Jazz Festival, France, 1985)
John Scofield – (Colchester UK, 1987)
Michael Brecker – (Fat Tuesday's, New York USA, 1987)
Little Feat / Neville Brothers – (Montreux Jazz Festival, Switzerland 1990)
Dr John – (House Of Blues, New Orleans USA, 1999)

Top 10 World Destinations

Tokyo, Japan
Oregon Coast, USA
Auckland & The Bay Of Islands, New Zealand
Daintree Rainforest, Northern Queensland, Australia
Kauai, Hawaii
New York City, USA
Bora Bora, French Polynesia
San Francisco & Bay Area, USA
Langkawi, Malaysia
Perugia, Italy

Top 10 Food

Sea Bass (in garlic crust)
Thai Green Curry (with sticky rice)
Crab Cakes (with plum sauce)
Fish n'Chips
Roast Chicken (with garlic mash & veg)
Corn Beef Hash (with poached eggs)
Louisiana White Chocolate Bread Pudding
New York Cheesecake
Buttermilk Pancakes (with maple syrup)
Dutch Apple Pie

TV Appearances, Recordings & Bibliography

<u>Anglia ITV 'Junior Angle Club'</u> (Mike Prior & the Escorts) August 1963

<u>BBC Film 'Hamburg Bound'</u> (Denny Raven & the Sabres) January 1964

<u>BBC Live Studio</u> (Denny Raven & the Sabres) March 1964

<u>Anglia ITV 'About Anglia'</u> (Denny Raven & The Sabres featuring Isabelle Bond) August 1964

<u>Live From The Top Ten Beat Club Vol 1</u> (Decca SLK 16330-P) Various Artists including Denny Raven & The Sabres (recorded Hamburg, Germany July 1964)

The Sabres EP (four track EP) (recorded Bayes Recording Studio October 1964) Also released on a limited edition CD (Various Artists) Shakers & Grovers (Parlazone Records EZCD8.02) www.eastzone.co.uk

The Barn Tapes (private recording) featuring B J Wilson, Pete Carter & Rick Meek (recorded B J Wilson Studio 1977/78)

Live At The Cross Keys (private recording) featuring George McKay, Nigel Portass, Pete Carter & Rick Meek (recorded November 1979)

Hamburg Days by Rick Meek *Blue Suede News #54* (Spring 2001) http://www.bluesuedenews.com

Procol Harum website www.procolharum.com

Other books of interest with reference to Hamburg & the 60's.

Hamburg (The Cradle Of Rock) – by Alan Clayson (Sanctury).
Beat Merchants – by Alan Clayson (Blandford)
Procul Harum (Beyond The Pale) – by Claes Johansen (SAF)
Travelling Man (On The Road With The Searchers) – by Frank Allen (Aureus)
Ginger Geezer (The Life of Vivian Stanshall) – by Lucian Randall & Chris Welch (4thestate)
All The Rage – by Ian 'Mac' McLagan (Pan)
Joe Cocker (The Authorised Biography) – by J P Bean (Virgin)
The Sensational Alex Harvey – by John Neil Munro (Firefly)
Graham Bond (The Mighty Shadow) – by Harry Shapiro (Guiness)

Photo Credits

Goodchild (Snettisham Hill Billy Band)
John Norman (Mike Prior & The Escorts)
Wolf Holtgreve (Sabres in Hamburg)
Lynn News (Sabres, Press Cuttings & ESP)
Eastern Evening News (Sabres Cartoon)
Goodchild (Three Piece Sweet & Ricky Allen)
Eastern Daily Press (52nd Street)
Bob Booth (Sabres recording)
Sue Wilson (Procol Harum)
Roy Williamson (Maureen & The Three Piece Sweet)
Dick Atkinson (In Memory of B J & B J in London)
Mary Relph (Some of the old gang)
Blue Suede News (Hamburg Story)
Ken Leyland (Rick fooling around at Nice)

Book title and cover layout from an idea by Kingsley Harris & Liz Farrow (East Anglian Music Archive)

Back Cover - Rick in Chicago 1993

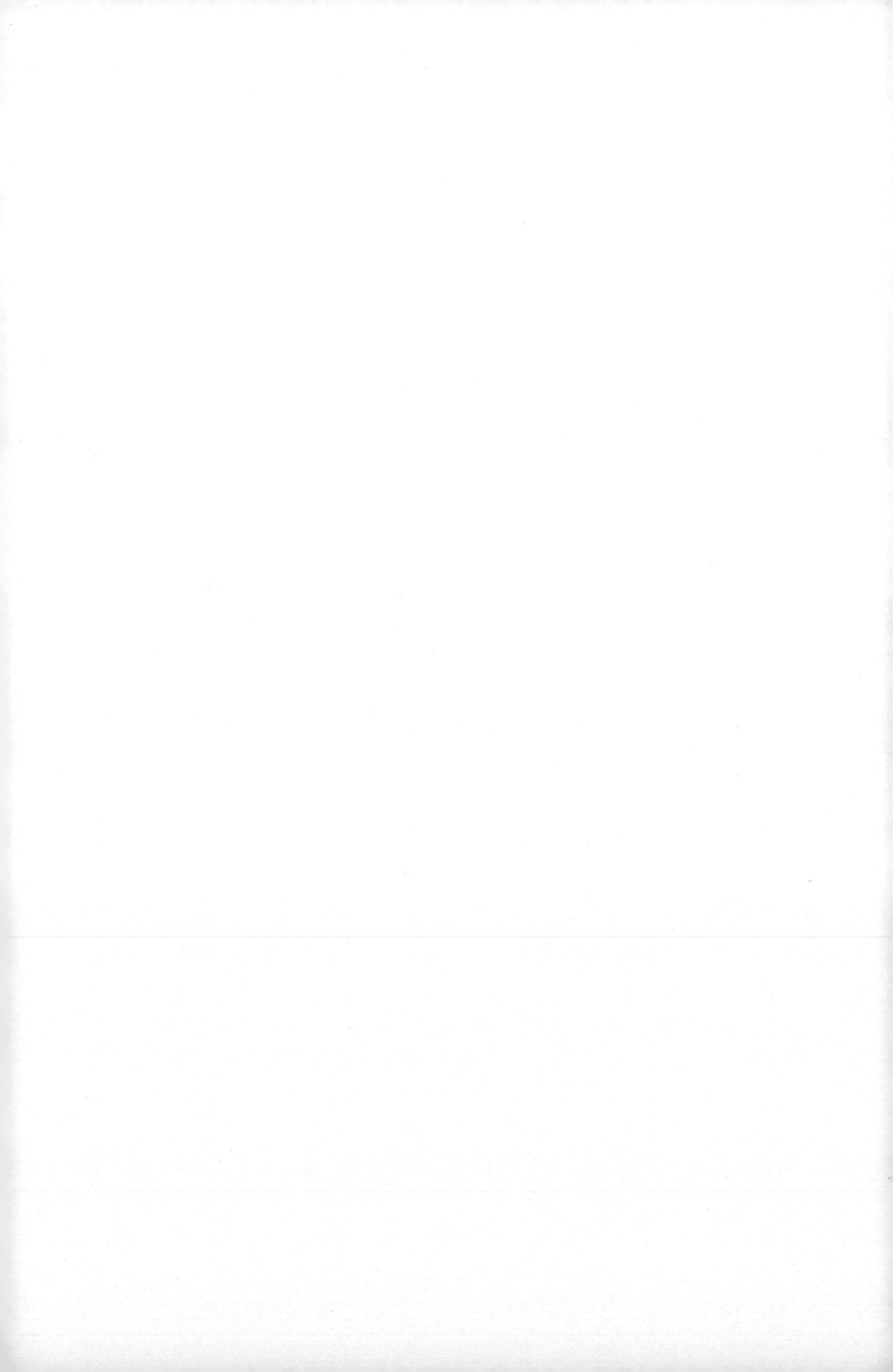